OPPOSING
VIEWPOINTS®
SERIES

The Catholic Church

Other Books of Related Interest:

Opposing Viewpoints Series

Anti-Semitism

Religious Liberty

Tibet

World Peace

At Issue Series

Are Abortion Rights Threatened?

Polygamy

Right to Die

Current Controversies Series

Abortion

Politics and Religion

Same-Sex Marriage

"Congress shall make
no law . . . abridging
the freedom of speech,
or of the press."

First Amendment to the US Constitution

The basic foundation of our democracy is the First Amendment guarantee of freedom of expression. The Opposing Viewpoints series is dedicated to the concept of this basic freedom and the idea that it is more important to practice it than to enshrine it.

The Catholic Church

Michael Ruth, Book Editor

GREENHAVEN PRESS
A part of Gale, Cengage Learning

Farmington Hills, Mich • San Francisco • New York • Waterville, Maine
Meriden, Conn • Mason, Ohio • Chicago

Judy Galens, *Manager, Frontlist Acquisitions*

© 2016 Greenhaven Press, a part of Gale, Cengage Learning.

Gale and Greenhaven Press are registered trademarks used herein under license.

For more information, contact:
Greenhaven Press
27500 Drake Rd.
Farmington Hills, MI 48331-3535
Or you can visit our Internet site at gale.cengage.com

For product information and technology assistance, contact us at

Gale Customer Support, 1-800-877-4253
For permission to use material from this text or product, submit all requests online at www.cengage.com/permissions

Further permissions questions can be emailed to permissionrequest@cengage.com

Articles in Greenhaven Press anthologies are often edited for length to meet page requirements. In addition, original titles of these works are changed to clearly present the main thesis and to explicitly indicate the author's opinion. Every effort is made to ensure that Greenhaven Press accurately reflects the original intent of the authors. Every effort has been made to trace the owners of copyrighted material.

Cover Image copyright © Ferenc Szelepcsenyi/Shutterstock.com.

LIBRARY OF CONGRESS CATALOGING-IN-PUBLICATION DATA

The Catholic Church / Michael Ruth, book editor.
    pages cm. -- -- (Opposing viewpoints)
    Includes bibliographical references and index.
    ISBN 978-0-7377-7538-9 (hardcover) -- ISBN 978-0-7377-7539-6 (pbk.)
    1. Catholic Church--Doctrines. I. Ruth, Michael, editor.
    BX1751.3.C377 2015
    282--dc23
                                2015024212

Printed in Mexico
1 2 3 4 5 6 7 19 18 17 16 15

Contents

Why Consider Opposing Viewpoints?   11

Introduction   14

Chapter 1: What Is the Catholic Church's Stance on Homosexuality?

Chapter Preface   19

1. Pope Francis's Welcoming of Gay People Creates   22
   Many Positive Opportunities
   Francis DeBernardo

2. Pope Francis Strays from Catholic Doctrine   27
   by Welcoming Gay People
   Raymond Leo Burke

3. The Catholic Church Should Never Recognize   32
   Same-Sex Marriages
   Thomas J. Paprocki

4. Catholics Can Embrace Same-Sex Marriage   39
   Without Compromising Their Faith
   Larry Donnelly

5. Catholic Institutions Should Not Be Forced   45
   to Hire Gay People
   John Zmirak

6. Catholic Leadership Should Stop Discriminating   51
   Against Gay People
   Taboola

7. Should the Catholic Church Ordain Gay Priests?   57
   Michael Brown

8. The Catholic Church Should Not Discriminate   63
   Against Gay Priests
   James Martin

Periodical and Internet Sources Bibliography   70

Chapter 2: What Role Does the Catholic Church Play in Health Issues?

Chapter Preface   72

1. Obamacare Discriminates Against Catholicism   74
   and Other Religions
   L. Martin Nussbaum

2. Catholics Should Not Use Arguments Based   80
   on Moral Reasoning Against Obamacare
   Thomas Farrell

3. Catholics Should View Abortion as a Moral Evil   86
   Richard M. Doerflinger

4. Pro-Choice Catholics Play an Important   90
   Role in the Abortion Debate
   Patricia Miller

5. Pope Francis's Comments on Family Planning   95
   Are Misguided
   Tara Culp-Ressler

6. Pope Francis Is Correct to Encourage   101
   Conservative Family Planning
   Tyler Anderson

7. Death with Dignity Opposes Catholic Teaching   106
   Donald Hanson

8. Catholics Should Not Oppose Death   110
   with Dignity
   Robert Olvera

Periodical and Internet Sources Bibliography   114

Chapter 3: What Are Issues Facing the Catholic Priesthood?

Chapter Preface   116

1. Catholic Priests Should Remain Celibate   118
   Stephen Beale

2. Catholic Priests Should Be Allowed to Marry   **123**
Dan Delzell

3. Women Should Never Be Ordained   **128**
Catholic Priests
Dwight Longenecker

4. Women Should Be Allowed to Become   **136**
Catholic Priests
Jo Piazza

5. Catholic Church's Stance Against Clerical   **141**
Abuse Not Enough
Lauren Carasik

6. The Catholic Church Is Progressing Toward   **147**
Clerical Abuse Reform
Priyanka Boghani

Periodical and Internet Sources Bibliography   **152**

Chapter 4: How Should the Catholic Church Interact with the Secular World?

Chapter Preface   **154**

1. The Catholic Church Should Participate   **156**
in Politics
Keith Fournier

2. How Pope Francis Allows Politics to Distort   **164**
the Christian Faith
Michael Brendan Dougherty

3. Pope Francis Is Correct on New   **169**
American-Cuban Relations
William R. Wineke

4. Cuban Dissident Voices and Pope Francis's   **173**
Deaf Ears
Nicholas G. Hahn III

5. Pope Francis Is Wrong to Combat   177
   Climate Change
   Marc Morano

6. Pope Francis Displays Sound Ethics   181
   in Combating Climate Change
   Rmuse

7. Pope Francis Is Wrong to Support Big Bang   188
   and Evolution
   Ken Ham

8. Pope Francis's Big Bang and Evolution Support   193
   Aligns with Catholicism
   Thomas Lucente

Periodical and Internet Sources Bibliography   198

For Further Discussion   199

Organizations to Contact   202

Bibliography of Books   208

Index   212

Why Consider Opposing Viewpoints?

> *"The only way in which a human being can make some approach to knowing the whole of a subject is by hearing what can be said about it by persons of every variety of opinion and studying all modes in which it can be looked at by every character of mind. No wise man ever acquired his wisdom in any mode but this."*
>
> *John Stuart Mill*

In our media-intensive culture it is not difficult to find differing opinions. Thousands of newspapers and magazines and dozens of radio and television talk shows resound with differing points of view. The difficulty lies in deciding which opinion to agree with and which "experts" seem the most credible. The more inundated we become with differing opinions and claims, the more essential it is to hone critical reading and thinking skills to evaluate these ideas. Opposing Viewpoints books address this problem directly by presenting stimulating debates that can be used to enhance and teach these skills. The varied opinions contained in each book examine many different aspects of a single issue. While examining these conveniently edited opposing views, readers can develop critical thinking skills such as the ability to compare and contrast authors' credibility, facts, argumentation styles, use of persuasive techniques, and other stylistic tools. In short, the Opposing Viewpoints Series is an ideal way to attain the higher-level thinking and reading skills so essential in a culture of diverse and contradictory opinions.

In addition to providing a tool for critical thinking, Opposing Viewpoints books challenge readers to question their own strongly held opinions and assumptions. Most people form their opinions on the basis of upbringing, peer pressure, and personal, cultural, or professional bias. By reading carefully balanced opposing views, readers must directly confront new ideas as well as the opinions of those with whom they disagree. This is not to argue simplistically that everyone who reads opposing views will—or should—change his or her opinion. Instead, the series enhances readers' understanding of their own views by encouraging confrontation with opposing ideas. Careful examination of others' views can lead to the readers' understanding of the logical inconsistencies in their own opinions, perspective on why they hold an opinion, and the consideration of the possibility that their opinion requires further evaluation.

Evaluating Other Opinions

To ensure that this type of examination occurs, Opposing Viewpoints books present all types of opinions. Prominent spokespeople on different sides of each issue as well as well-known professionals from many disciplines challenge the reader. An additional goal of the series is to provide a forum for other, less known, or even unpopular viewpoints. The opinion of an ordinary person who has had to make the decision to cut off life support from a terminally ill relative, for example, may be just as valuable and provide just as much insight as a medical ethicist's professional opinion. The editors have two additional purposes in including these less known views. One, the editors encourage readers to respect others' opinions—even when not enhanced by professional credibility. It is only by reading or listening to and objectively evaluating others' ideas that one can determine whether they are worthy of consideration. Two, the inclusion of such viewpoints encourages the important critical thinking skill of objectively evaluating an author's credentials and bias. This evaluation will illuminate an author's reasons for taking a particular stance on an issue and will aid in readers' evaluation of the author's ideas.

It is our hope that these books will give readers a deeper understanding of the issues debated and an appreciation of the complexity of even seemingly simple issues when good and honest people disagree. This awareness is particularly important in a democratic society such as ours in which people enter into public debate to determine the common good. Those with whom one disagrees should not be regarded as enemies but rather as people whose views deserve careful examination and may shed light on one's own.

Thomas Jefferson once said that "difference of opinion leads to inquiry, and inquiry to truth." Jefferson, a broadly educated man, argued that "if a nation expects to be ignorant and free . . . it expects what never was and never will be." As individuals and as a nation, it is imperative that we consider the opinions of others and examine them with skill and discernment. The Opposing Viewpoints series is intended to help readers achieve this goal.

David L. Bender and Bruno Leone,
Founders

Introduction

> "*The Catholic Church, operating on the doctrine that she is the continuing presence and ministry of Jesus Christ on earth, has always said both a 'yes' and a 'no' to the power of government.*"
>
> —Frank Pavone,
> "*Too Much—or Too Little—Catholic Influence in Politics?,*"
> *FaithStreet.com, March 27, 2012*

With 1.2 billion followers, Catholicism is the largest denomination of Christianity, which itself is the largest religion in the world, boasting 2.2 billion adherents. Based in Vatican City, an autonomous city-state located within the borders of Rome, Italy, the Catholic Church is headed by the pope and ministered throughout the world by a hierarchy of cardinals, bishops, priests, deacons, and laypeople. Today the Catholic Church is primarily a religious organization that occasionally presents its own views on matters of politics and government. Throughout its sometimes tumultuous two thousand–year history, however, the church has entered and actively shaped numerous areas of the secular sphere.

Christianity was founded throughout the mid to late first century AD, mainly by the twelve apostles of Jesus Christ, on whose life and teachings the doctrines of the Christian church are based. After Jesus's death at the hands of the Jewish and Roman authorities of ancient Palestine, his followers scattered to Christianize numerous regions of the Middle East, Western Asia, and North Africa.

The early Christians were all-inclusive in teaching others about Jesus's oneness with God, his proclamations of love and forgiveness as necessary criteria to enter heaven, and his absolute power to save the souls of humanity from eternal damnation after death. The Christians discriminated against no one and welcomed both Jewish and non-Jewish converts to Christianity. It was in this way that early Christianity soon began taking on a distinctly Catholic flavor. Descending from the Greek word *katholikos*, the word *catholic* refers to the quality of universality and openness. The Christian denomination that would ultimately become Catholicism formed in the later 100s and 200s, as bishops began establishing what they determined to be the correct sources of theological authority, which included the Scriptures, the churches, and the tradition of faith.

Catholics would also look to a pope to lead their church. Beginning with Peter, an apostle of Jesus, the papacy was created as a successive line of Jesus's elected representatives on Earth. Since the first century, the popes had been based in Rome as the bishops of the city, but their religious influence was overshadowed by the powerful Roman emperor. In 330, however, the emperor Constantine relocated the capital of the Roman Empire to Constantinople, leaving the papacy to flourish in Rome, a city Catholics associated with religious and political supremacy. Thus, Roman Catholicism became the preeminent branch of Christianity in the West, while those Christians who disagreed with the Catholic sources of theological authority and disapproved of the power of the papacy formed the Orthodox Christian church in the East.

Almost since its inception, the Catholic Church was nearly as much a political institution as a religious one. The early medieval period of the 400s and 500s saw popes sending representatives to convert various distant lands, such as England, to Christianity. Meanwhile, back in Rome, the popes held various councils to broaden the church's rule abroad and increase the power of the papacy. The church still held great political sway half a millennium later, when, in 1095, Pope Urban II declared war against the Muslims who had by that point captured and occupied Jerusalem, a city highly regarded by Christians as the place of Jesus's death. This began the two hundred–year Crusades, a series of holy wars waged between Christians and Muslims for dominance of the Holy Land. By the end of the wars, Jerusalem remained in Muslim control.

The Catholic Church began exerting its secular influence again in 1233 with its implementation of the Medieval Inquisition. This was Pope Gregory IX's effort to eradicate heresy, or untrue doctrine, from the church by establishing inquests meant to root out the offending ideas. The papal inquisitors thoroughly questioned and judged anyone accused of spreading heresy against the faith, and the convicted who refused to recant their beliefs were burned at the stake or imprisoned. Inquisitors also routinely tortured those only suspected of being heretics; this was intended to procure confessions, though many of these were lies told simply to avoid death.

In the late 1500s, the Catholic Church resurrected its inquisitional authority with the Roman Inquisition, a system of tribunals meant to suppress the growing influence of Protestantism. Protestantism was a new branch of Christianity started by German theologian Martin Luther as a rebellion against what he believed was the gross power and corruption of the Roman Catholic Church. Like the Medieval Inquisition before it, the Roman Inquisition tried and convicted most of those suspected of spreading false teachings within the church.

The Roman Inquisition embodied the Counter-Reformation, the Catholic Church's sixteenth- and seventeenth-century attempt to reestablish its religious authority after the Protestant Reformation had shaken the world's trust in the increasingly corrupt and overbearing papacy. The Counter-Reformation brought some new changes to Catholic practice but was mostly an endeavor to reclaim, through intimidation and violence, recent Catholic converts to Protestantism.

The papacy's resurgence was short-lived, however. Although the 1600s and 1700s were marked by a notable expansion of Catholicism in the Americas, the scientific revolution, the Age of Enlightenment, and the rise of absolutist European monarchies meant that the Catholic Church gradually lost its political influence as the early modern period became the modern era.

The Catholic Church in the twenty-first century wields no political power. However, this has not kept church leadership from lobbying for political issues relevant to the Catholic faith. After his election in 2013, Pope Francis stated that Catholics should vocally support pro-life initiatives by opposing abortion and contraception, aiding the poor, and working to reduce climate change. The world media noted that Francis's lobbying for these and other issues made him one of the most political popes of the modern age. Although the papacy has never again exercised the kind of political strength of its past, the Catholic Church continues to fashion itself as a religious haven dedicated to modeling the world according to its beliefs.

Opposing Viewpoints: The Catholic Church presents a range of questions relevant to the contemporary Catholic Church Authors from different religious and political persuasions attempt to answer these questions in chapters titled "What Is the Catholic Church's Stance on Homosexuality?," "What Role Does the Catholic Church Play in Health Issues?," "What Are Issues Facing the Catholic Priesthood?," and "How Should the Catholic Church Interact with the Secular World?"

CHAPTER 1

What Is the Catholic Church's Stance on Homosexuality?

Chapter Preface

The Catholic Church has historically been strongly opposed to all forms of homosexual behavior and acts, labeling such acts as grave sins against God. The church originally based this doctrine on various passages from the Old and New Testaments of the Bible that explicitly condemn such actions.

One of the most famous examples of this comes from chapter 19 of the Old Testament's book of Genesis, in which angels sent by God blind all the men of the city of Sodom for engaging in homosexual deeds; God himself later destroys the city by fire. In the New Testament, the commission of homosexual acts is denounced mostly in St. Paul's letters to members of the early church. In his first letter to the Corinthians, for example, Paul writes that no immoral person—including thieves, drunks, adulterers, and sexual deviants—will enter God's kingdom. He echoes this sentiment in his first letter to Timothy, in his letter to Jude, and in several of his other epistles.

These early writings formed a clear foundation for what the Catholic Church's permanent stance on homosexuality should be, and for the first two thousand years of the church's existence, none of the hundreds of popes wavered from these views. Homosexual acts remained affronts to God, and those who led these kinds of sinful lives, in the church's eyes, could not enter heaven.

Beginning in the second half of the twentieth century, however, the church began to encounter increasing resistance to its homosexuality dogma from members of the gay community. The church was labeled outdated, homophobic, and discriminatory for not affording gay people the same treatment it allotted to heterosexuals. In 1969 an advocacy group called DignityUSA formed in San Diego, California, as an alliance of gay and lesbian Catholics who felt ostracized by their own church. That same year's Stonewall riots, in which large groups of gay people in New York's Greenwich Village began violently protesting the police's raid of a local gay bar, are generally considered the inception of the gay rights movement in the United States.

By the early 1970s, the Catholic Church had begun to be affected by this growing unrest, with the National Federation of Priests' Councils and the National Coalition of American Nuns officially altering their organizations' doctrines to encourage American legislators to grant full civil rights to gay people. However, the changing opinions of certain members within the church did not reflect the position of church leadership in Vatican City, which declared in 1986—under Pope John Paul II—that although simply being gay was not a sin, engaging in homosexual acts remained a profound moral offense.

In 2013, however, the newly inaugurated Pope Francis shocked the Catholic world when he appeared to soften the church's view of homosexuality, saying that, even as pope, he was in no position to judge gay people who strived to adhere to Catholic teachings. At a church synod in late 2014, Francis proposed to his gathered bishops from around the world that the Catholic Church be more welcoming of gay people and invite them to use their unique spiritual gifts for church betterment. Despite his seemingly modernist views of homosexuality, however, Francis still aligned himself with all of his papal predecessors by continuing to decry same-sex marriage as immoral.

The following chapter presents arguments concerning numerous aspects of the Catholic Church's stance on homosexuality. These include the question of how greatly Pope Francis's welcoming of gay people to the church veers from previous Catholic doctrine, whether the church should accept same-sex marriage, what rights Catholic institutions have to reject gay people for employment, and whether openly gay men should be permitted to serve as priests.

| "If the gifts of gay and lesbian people are truly accepted, Catholicism will be forever changed."

Pope Francis's Welcoming of Gay People Creates Many Positive Opportunities

Francis DeBernardo

In the following viewpoint, Francis DeBernardo argues that Pope Francis's welcoming words to gay Catholics have fundamentally changed the Catholic Church's outlook on homosexuality. Although DeBernardo admits that the church still opposes same-sex marriage, he believes the pope's effort to integrate gay people into the church more fully is an important first step in repairing the historically tense relations between the Catholic Church and the gay community. To DeBernardo, this new participation in the church will allow gay people to grow closer to God. DeBernardo is the executive director of New Ways Ministry, a Catholic organization that works to improve the relationship between gay people and the Catholic Church.

As you read, consider the following questions:

1. DeBernardo suggests what four options for Catholic parishes and schools to include gay and lesbian people in their faith communities?

2. What does DeBernardo identify as a spiritual gift that gay people can acquire from telling the truth about themselves?

3. With whom does DeBernardo claim gay people can strengthen their relationships using sexuality as spiritual experiences?

The news from the Vatican that Catholic parishes should reach out more warmly to lesbian and gay people opens up a whole new era of discourse in the church concerning sexuality. The statement from church officials calls on Catholic communities to be "accepting and valuing" lesbian and gay people's sexual orientation and to recognize that lesbian and gay people "have gifts and qualities to offer to the Christian community."

These simple directions don't change doctrine about same-sex marriages, and the church's opposition to this social development still stands. But in fact, words like these are a total game changer. While a change in language and tone, but not of substance, may seem insignificant, this perspective misses the point that a change in language and tone is the necessary first step toward more substantial change in the Catholic Church.

This document and Pope Francis's many gay-affirming statements represent that first step. The language shift emboldens church ministers to change pastoral practice. Catholic parishes and schools can now take greater steps to include lesbian and gay people in their faith communities. This might include establishing faith sharing groups for LGBT [lesbian, gay, bisexual, and transgender] people, appointing lesbian and

US Catholics' Views on Homosexuality, Same-Sex Marriage

Homosexuality should be ...

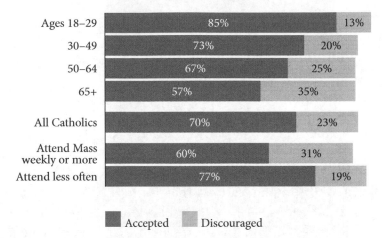

Ages 18–29	85% / 13%
30–49	73% / 20%
50–64	67% / 25%
65+	57% / 35%
All Catholics	70% / 23%
Attend Mass weekly or more	60% / 31%
Attend less often	77% / 19%

■ Accepted ■ Discouraged

Support for same-sex marriage

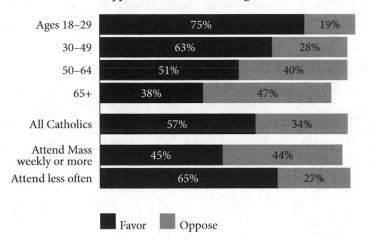

Ages 18–29	75% / 19%
30–49	63% / 28%
50–64	51% / 40%
65+	38% / 47%
All Catholics	57% / 34%
Attend Mass weekly or more	45% / 44%
Attend less often	65% / 27%

■ Favor ■ Oppose

Source: Acceptance of homosexuality from Pew Research Center survey conducted Jan. 23–March 16, 2014. Support for same-sex marriage from aggregated 2014 Pew Research surveys. "Neither/both equally" and "don't know/refused" responses omitted.

TAKEN FROM: Michael Lipka, "Young U.S. Catholics Overwhelmingly Accepting of Homosexuality," Pew Research Center, October 16, 2014.

gay people to leadership roles and visible ministries, including sexual orientation in educational programs, and involving the parish with gay community organizations that help vulnerable populations such as youth.

As pastoral practice develops, church leaders will become more familiar with lesbian and gay people and issues, ending the long unnatural silence in local church settings about LGBT topics. Fear of being reprimanded for being too gay-accepting kept pastoral ministers from even acknowledging that lesbian and gay people existed. The new language promises to change that fearful attitude, and it is very likely that we will see pastoral ministers begin much bolder initiatives.

Change in pastoral practice will eventually lead to change in doctrine. As church leaders reflect on the activities of their faith communities, they will see that the Christian message of love has come alive in this new outreach. Eventually, the doctrine will change. It's hard to put a timeline on such an enterprise. God moves in mysterious ways, and often on an even more mysterious schedule.

A Church Transformed

But the Vatican's new message holds the promise for even greater change than LGBT acceptance. Since Catholics are now being called to recognize the gifts that lesbian and gay people bring to the church, the church itself can be transformed. If the gifts of gay and lesbian people are truly accepted, Catholicism will be forever changed.

Many Catholic parishes and colleges have already been welcoming LGBT people into their midst for many years now. In addition to helping LGBT people, these institutions have themselves been transformed into more loving and just places. Why? Because LGBT people bring their unique spiritual journeys to the community, and all benefit from their insights and perspectives. Because LGBT people have had to face up to difficult odds to come to self-awareness and self-acceptance, their spiritual journeys produce powerful traits from which the whole community can benefit. For example, because LGBT people have had to learn how to recognize the truth about their identities, usually in the face of great social pressure, they often have the gift of being courageous truth tellers. The Catholic community badly needs the ability to tell the truth, as the clerical sexual abuse crisis has shown.

Another spiritual gift that comes from this truth telling is the gift of self-love. Because negative messages encourage LGBT people to hate themselves, they develop a strong sense of self-love to counter these earlier feelings. This self-love is not a selfish idea, but a healthy and holy assessment of one's strengths and weaknesses. Self-acceptance often helps to propagate the wonderful sense of humor that we see in the LGBT community: the ability to laugh at one's foibles. A more humorous church would be a blessing!

Similarly, LGBT people often recognize the intimate connection between sexuality and spirituality. Because recognizing the goodness of human longings and desires to give and receive love has sometimes been a struggle, LGBT people often perceive that sexuality is a spiritual experience that not only strengthens relationships between persons but also with God. This insight is a gift that other people in the church—heterosexuals, young people, older people, married, single, and celibate—need desperately.

Though the new Vatican document is still a work in progress, which will be debated both this week [in October 2014] and in the coming year, this version reveals that a strong current of gay-affirmative thinking exists among some very highly placed church officials—something that was not evident even just a week ago. These leaders will certainly be working to maintain this spirit of inclusion, and, perhaps even to strengthen it. Both the Catholic Church and the LGBT community will benefit from such a partnership.

| *"It seems to [many] that the ship of the church has lost its compass."*

Pope Francis Strays from Catholic Doctrine by Welcoming Gay People

Raymond Leo Burke

In the following viewpoint, Raymond Leo Burke laments and criticizes some of the Catholic Church's changing positions on issues of sexuality. These include a proposed openness to cohabitating couples, adulterers, and gay people who engage in homosexual behavior. Burke contends that a strong, traditionalist Catholic stance cannot accept such acts as anything less than grave sins against God. He also argues that Pope Francis's acceptance of gay Catholics has created ambiguity as to whether the Catholic Church is losing its focus in the modern era. Burke is an American cardinal of the Catholic Church currently serving as patron of the Sovereign Military Order of Malta.

As you read, consider the following questions:

1. What does Burke identify as a doctrinal error he found in the synod's Relatio post disceptationem?

2. What words does Burke use to describe why the Catholic Church considers homosexual acts to be evil?

3. What four areas does Burke name as being constant traditions on which Catholics can rely?

US Cardinal Raymond Leo Burke is considered one of the representatives of the Curial sector most resistant to change, as he demonstrates by deeming "critical" the current moment, in which for "many" the church is sailing "as a ship without a rudder." Opposed to the theses of Cardinal Walter Kasper on the admission of the remarried divorced to the sacraments—"marriage is indissoluble. If I marry someone, I cannot live with someone else"—he calls homosexuality "suffering" and he considers that there was an intent to conduct the Synod on the Family [a meeting of bishops to discuss problems facing families] towards a position of laxity. He even denounced the "manipulation" that was tried with the information that was released from the synodal assembly, at the same time in which he laments the "confusion" and the "pastoral difficulties" caused by the debate on these hot-button issues. Prefect of the Supreme Tribunal of the Apostolic Signatura, the Vatican Supreme Court, his transferal to the position of cardinal patron of the Order of Malta, an honorific job without any content, is considered certain.

What is the feeling that the synod left you? Was there confrontation?

There was an open and strong discussion. In the past, the interventions of the synodal fathers were always published, but not now. All the information came from the summaries of Fr. [Federico] Lombardi and the conferences he organized with the press. These summaries surprised me. They did not reflect well the content of the discussions; they gave the impression that all was moving in favor of the position exposed by Cardinal [Walter] Kasper.

The real shock came about with the Relatio post disceptationem [the summary of the interventions of the first week of the synod]. It looked like a manifesto to change the discipline of the church concerning irregular unions. They offered a greater opening to couples who cohabit without the sacrament of matrimony and to persons who suffer with the homosexual condition.

Did the other synodal fathers share your rejection?

Indeed. All of us in my minor circle [small discussion group] were surprised. We spent a lot of time basing the final document in Sacred Scripture and the Magisterium [teaching authority of the church]. Errors had to be corrected: For example, the one that positive elements can be found in sinful acts, as cohabitation, adultery, or in sexual acts between persons suffering of the homosexual condition. This confusion was too grave. We made the effort so that the beauty that the matrimonial state as an indissoluble union, that is faithful and destined to procreation created by God, could reemerge. Faced with difficult situations, we distinguish between love for the sinner and hatred for sin. We, the moderators and rapporteurs of the minor circles, asked for our works to be published. Until then, the public did not know what we thought. Everything was controlled and manipulated, if I may say so. . . .

Grave Pastoral Difficulties

Another hot-button issue is that of homosexuals. You mentioned them before as "persons who suffer from a homosexual condition." Do you see it as a malady?

It is a suffering. God did not create us so that man be with man, and woman with woman. This is clear from our very nature. We are made for heterosexual union, for marriage. I refuse to speak of homosexual persons, because nobody identifies by this tendency. It is a person that has this tendency, which is a suffering.

What did it seem to you when the pope said that who was he to judge a gay person?

He said that he cannot judge the person before God, whatever may be his culpability. But the acts themselves must be judged; I do not believe that the pope thinks in a different way. [The acts] are sinful and counter-natural. The pope has never said that we can find positive elements in them. It is impossible to find positive elements in an evil act.

[Pope] Francis spoke in his final message to the synod of a "hostile rigidity" and he lamented that some close themselves "within what is written" without allowing themselves to be "surprised by God." How do you interpret his words?

It is difficult. They can be interpreted in the sense that doctrine and discipline are opposed to the action of the Holy Spirit. This is not the Catholic way of thinking. Doctrine and discipline are the conditions for a true encounter with Christ. I have heard many saying that the pope does not want to insist on discipline nor on doctrine. It is not the adequate interpretation of his words.

Some faithful are concerned with the path that the church has taken. What do you say to them?

Many have shown me this concern. In such a critical moment, in which is a strong feeling that the church is as a ship without a rudder, the reason does not matter; it is more important than ever to study our faith, to have sane spiritual guidance, and to give strong witness of the faith. Some tell me, for instance, that taking part in the pro-life movement is not important anymore. I tell them that it is more important than ever.

Do you see the church as being in a moment in which there is no one in charge?

I have all the respect for the Petrine [referring to Peter, the first pope] ministry, and I do not want it to appear like I am a voice opposed to the pope. I would like to be a teacher of the faith, with all my weaknesses, saying the truth that many feel today. They feel a bit of seasickness, because it seems to them that the ship of the church has lost its compass. The cause of this disorientation must be put aside. We have the constant tradition of the church, the teachings, the liturgy, morals. The catechism does not change.

"Couples of the same sex lack the capacity to realize the goods of natural marriage for the simple reason that they lack the complementarity of male and female."

The Catholic Church Should Never Recognize Same-Sex Marriages

Thomas J. Paprocki

In the following viewpoint, Thomas J. Paprocki argues that Catholics should view same-sex marriage as illegitimate because it cannot replicate the natural male-female partnership of heterosexual marriage. In Paprocki's view, making same-sex marriage legal would allow it to take place physically but would still be absent of any kind of morality or adherence to natural law. Paprocki also argues that marriage is a union that is meant to produce children for the continuance of society, and he rejects same-sex marriage because it is incapable of doing this. Paprocki is bishop of the Diocese of Springfield in Illinois. He is the author of the book Holy Goals for Body and Soul: Eight Steps to Connect Sports with God and Faith.

As you read, consider the following questions:

1. What does Paprocki say is the origin of marriage?

2. What does Paprocki identify as the state's role in creating laws for marriage?

3. What does Paprocki claim is the first cell of society?

In the light of popular opinion today, I recognize that I have an uphill struggle to persuade people of the reasons why same-sex relationships should not be legally recognized as marriages.

Yet, the ethical or moral analysis of an issue is not properly based on polls or surveys of public opinion, but on values, virtues and principles. The challenge is first to show what marriage is and why it deserves a unique status. . . .

In my remarks tonight [on May 31, 2013] I will address the claims of an argument against my views that would go something like this:

> The Catholic Church teaches that marriage is limited to the union of one man and one woman and that the civil law should reflect this definition. Some non-Catholic religions, and some people with no religious affiliation, are supportive of homosexual marriage. The civil law governs a diverse and pluralistic society, and it is not legitimate to single out one religious group's views and grant them favored status by enacting their religious views into law. Therefore, it is not legitimate for civil society to limit marriage to heterosexual couples.

The first thing to note in response to this argument is that it relies on several false premises. The Catholic Church did not invent marriage as an institution limited to heterosexual couples. Neither did the state. Marriage is a pre-political and natural phenomenon that arises out of the nature of human beings. The Catholic Church, along with virtually every religion and culture in the world, recognizes and supports this natural institution because without it, no society will exist or flourish. I will discuss this phenomenon shortly. . . .

First, I will discuss the nature of marriage as a natural institution; second, I will argue that civil law and a limited government act beyond their competence and authority when they attempt to redefine the fundamental attributes of marriage.

The Nature of Marriage

First, neither the state nor the church "created" marriage. Marriage is a natural outgrowth of human nature, capacities and needs in a similar way that language is a natural outgrowth of human nature, capacities and needs. No one at the dawn of time sat down with a committee of linguists to develop languages, nor did a blue-ribbon committee of sociologists and politicians create marriage.

Marriage grows out of a natural affinity and complementarity of male and female—in other words, the ways in which one gender completes the other emotionally, spiritually and physically. Most of our natural inclinations can be developed and accomplished through our own efforts—we can fulfill our inclinations toward preserving our health, satisfying our hunger, learning the truth, seeking the beautiful, through our own solitary efforts. Even if others assist us in reaching these goals, it is our own efforts that ultimately are determinative of our fulfillment. But the inclination, natural desire and capacity toward procreation and creation of a family can only be fulfilled through the union of a man and woman. Even though new biotech interventions in reproduction have advanced seemingly solitary avenues to this fulfillment, say through artificial reproduction, they all must find ways to mimic the union of a man and woman in order to be successful.

The inclination toward these goods is obviously keenly felt by all human beings, including those with same-sex attractions. But couples of the same sex lack the capacity to realize the goods of natural marriage for the simple reason that they lack the complementarity of male and female. . . .

Law, Truth and Marriage

Next, I would like to turn to a consideration of the proper relationship between law and truth, or, more specifically, between law and the truth about marriage as held on the basis of natural law reasoning. . . .

A re-definition of marriage to include same-sex marriage is beyond the competence of the state, because marriage both precedes the state and is a necessary condition for the continuation of the state (because future generations arise from and are formed in marriage). When a state enacts a law saying that a same-sex relationship can constitute a marriage, it has the power to enforce that in a society's external practices, but it is devoid of any intrinsic moral legitimacy and is contrary to any natural reality. If the government says that an apple is now the same as an orange, and the law requires everyone to call apples "oranges," the state would have the power to punish anyone who calls an apple an "apple" instead of an "orange," but it would be a totalitarian abuse of raw power and would not change the biological reality of the nature of the fruit in question. So too with the definition of marriage. . . .

The state has a duty to preserve and promote marriage as an institution that precedes the state, but the state does not have the authority to fundamentally redefine the nature of that institution. Similarly, the state has the authority to enact the "rules of the road" to protect vehicle drivers. But it has no authority or power to change the laws of physics so that car crashes will be less destructive. Rather the state assesses the preexisting factors that influence safe driving—the age when most persons can handle the responsibility of driving, the effect of alcohol on drivers, the best way to construct roadways,

Where Major Religions Stand on Same-Sex Marriage

Sanctions Same-Sex Marriage	Prohibits Same-Sex Marriage	No Clear Position
Episcopal Church	American Baptist Churches	Buddhism
Presbyterian Church (USA)	Church of Jesus Christ of Latter-day Saints (Mormon)	Hinduism
Conservative Jewish Movement	Islam	
Reform Jewish Movement	Lutheran Church–Missouri Synod	
Society of Friends (Quaker)	Orthodox Jewish Movement	
Unitarian Universalist Association of Churches	Roman Catholic Church	
United Church of Christ	Southern Baptist Convention	
Evangelical Lutheran Church in America	United Methodist Church	

TAKEN FROM: David Masci and Michael Lipka, "Where Christian Churches, Other Religions Stand on Gay Marriage," Pew Research Center, July 2, 2015.

maximum safe speeds—in order to create rules that best accord with these preexisting realities. The same should be true of marriage.

The benefits and duties conferred on marriage simply respond to the reality that the state cannot exist without families who will bring into existence the next generations. Those who advance a view of the family that is subordinate to and dependent upon the state for its existence turn the relationship of the family and state upside down. The family itself is the first cell of society, from which the state receives its existence. In a very real sense, the state exists to serve the family, which has its own legitimate nature and identity. It is not within the power of the state, particularly a state which claims to embrace the notion of a limited government, to redefine marriage in order to advance the state's interests in equality of treatment. . . .

If you acknowledge that truth exists, then we can discuss and even argue about whether or not I or the Catholic Church correctly understands the truth of this matter. But if you deny that there is such a thing as truth, that is, *the* truth, not just *my* truth and *your* truth, then the matter becomes merely an exercise of raw political power in terms of who has more votes to impose an agenda, and that is what makes it ultimately tyrannical. . . .

I conclude by recalling St. Paul's visit to Athens. We read in the Acts of the Apostles that Paul engaged in daily debates in the public square with ordinary passers-by. Some Epicurean and Stoic philosophers disputed with him, some of them asking, "What is this magpie trying to say to us?" (Acts 17:18). Perhaps you are asking the same thing of me right now! After Paul addressed the Athenian citizens in the Areopagus, we are told that "some sneered, while others said, 'We must hear you on this topic some other time'" (Acts 17:32). Again, some of you may be sneering, and I might be lucky if you said you were willing to hear me again on this topic some other time.

But the passage ends by saying that a "few did join him, however, and became believers" (Acts 17:34). In the end, I hope that at least a few of you will agree with my remarks.

| "*Getting married to someone I love made me far more receptive to listening to same-sex couples who were denied the same right.*"

Catholics Can Embrace Same-Sex Marriage Without Compromising Their Faith

Larry Donnelly

In the following viewpoint, Larry Donnelly argues that Catholics would not be sinning against their faith if they supported marriage equality for gay and lesbian people. He chronicles his own transition from opposing same-sex marriage to supporting it, claiming his Catholic faith was responsible for each view. Donnelly describes the factors that changed his mind, arguing that heterosexual couples who value their own marriages should be able to stand in solidarity with same-sex partners who also wish to get married. Donnelly works as an attorney in Boston, Massachusetts. He writes for TheJournal.ie and IrishCentral.com.

As you read, consider the following questions:

1. Which two public figures does Donnelly cite as examples of the changing public opinion on gay marriage in the United States?

2. What were the proposed negative consequences of legal-izing gay marriage in Massachusetts that Donnelly says did not come true?

3. What does Donnelly say happened in Massachusetts in 2007 that allowed gay marriage to become fully imple-mented there?

On Friday, the 22nd of May 2015, the Irish electorate will go to the polls and be asked to approve or reject the fol-lowing sentence: "Marriage may be contracted in accordance with law by two persons without distinction as to their sex." I am in favour of this proposition and will be voting Yes to marriage equality for gay and lesbian couples.

While a clear majority of Irish people in my age group, and nearly all of my colleagues in legal academia, likely ar-rived at this conclusion quickly and instinctively, I can't say that this has been the case for me. Ten years ago, even five years ago, my support extended only to civil partnerships for same-sex couples. When questioned, I repeatedly and reso-lutely argued that marriage was exclusively the union of one man and one woman.

My position was rooted in the Catholic faith I am still proud to practice and in a stubborn refusal to acknowledge that a civil marriage shouldn't be defined by the tenets of my religion.

A Seismic Shift

I was not alone in failing to identify what's oft been termed the "civil rights issue of our generation." President [Bill] Clin-ton, who infamously signed the (since partially repealed) De-fense of Marriage Act prohibiting the recognition by the fed-eral government of any same-sex marriage authorised by a state, and President [Barack] Obama both initially opposed the right of gay and lesbian couples to marry before endorsing marriage equality. Although political considerations have surely played a part in informing their former and present stances, their evolution on the issue is mirrored by a seismic shift in public opinion and in the law with respect to access to marriage.

In 2003, surveys showed that only about a third of Americans believed that gay and lesbian people should be allowed to marry someone of the same sex. Opinion polls taken during the first two months of 2015 reveal that that level of support has almost doubled. At least 60% of adults in the US believe in marriage equality. My native Massachusetts became the first state to legalise same-sex marriage in 2003 via a decision of our Supreme Judicial Court. 36 other states now permit it, with much of the change in the law having taken place in the past two years.

A significant amount has been written about why this sea change has occurred in the US and elsewhere. It's probably impossible to delineate all of the myriad reasons behind a very real movement of hearts and minds. However, I can attest as to why my own view has changed.

Alarmists Proved Wrong

First, none of the dire consequences of marriage equality foretold by the naysayers have been visited upon Massachusetts since 2003. In the wake of the court ruling, these (mainly outside) groups and individuals claimed that fewer people would marry; that fewer children would be raised by a married mother and father; that more children would grow up fatherless; that birth rates would fall; that fewer people would remain monogamous and sexually faithful; and that there would be demands for legalisation of polygamy.

These alarmist assertions have, for the most part, proven wildly inaccurate. And where the naysayers haven't been totally wrong, the trends in Massachusetts are entirely consistent with what's happened nationally. Furthermore, it is interesting that a number of the arguments against marriage equality in

Massachusetts were, just as they are in Ireland in 2015, child centric. Yet there is not one shred of evidence that children have suffered or been disadvantaged in any way since 2003.

The fact that same-sex marriage resulted from a judicial decision was another ground for objection. We lawyers have an array of different perspectives on when judicial interpretation crosses the line and becomes judicial lawmaking. Most of us can agree, however, that it is typically better for issues involving profound moral questions to be resolved by the broader citizenry or their representatives, rather than by un-elected judges. As such, it is ideal that the voters of Ireland will decide on marriage equality. And this objection in Massachusetts was fully vitiated in 2007, when the state legislature refused to approve an anti-same-sex marriage constitutional amendment.

But beyond the statistics and political and judicial wrangling, something far more important transpired in Massachusetts. Same-sex couples got married. It was no big deal. The sky did not fall in. Theirs remain a very small percentage of the overall number of marriages. Marriage equality did not affect existing marriages, nor did it stop tens of thousands of heterosexual couples from taking the plunge. It became settled law and a fact of life, and people have moved on.

Empathy Toward Same-Sex Couples

The second thing that helped to change my view was my own marriage. Getting married to someone I love made me far more receptive to listening to same-sex couples who were denied the same right. Their personal stories are heartrending and compelling.

My religion discerns a difference between their love and the love between me and my wife. The Catholic Church has the right, which I would defend, to recognise and perform marriages only between persons of the opposite sex. The more I've thought about it, though, especially in light of the realities

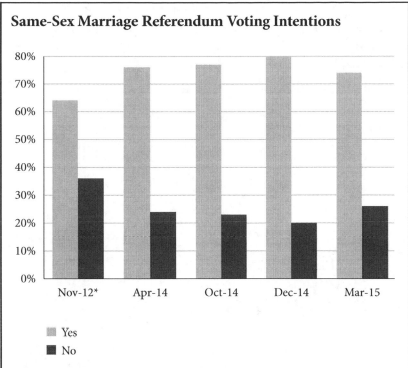

Same-Sex Marriage Referendum Voting Intentions

2014 Question: "There will be a referendum on same-sex marriage next year. Will you vote 'Yes' to allow same-sex marriage or 'No' not to allow same-sex marriage?"
2015 Question: "Two referendums will be held on May 22nd, the first one is on same-sex marriage. Will you vote 'Yes' to allow same-sex marriage*or 'No' not to allow same-sex marriage?"
*Question context differs: 2012 question was asked in a battery of other referendums as part of Changing Ireland Survey.

TAKEN FROM: Stephen Collins, "Poll Finds Drop in Support for Same-Sex Marriage," *Irish Times*, March 27, 2015.

of Western society in 2015, I can see no valid justification for a government to similarly differentiate and deny its citizens equality of access to civil marriage on this basis.

I can empathise with voters who just aren't sure about the forthcoming referendum. I can understand why some get irritated by over-the-top criticisms of the church, or intimations that a No vote would make Ireland appear "backward," or a sense that this is a project for an elite who don't really care about the more mundane struggles individuals and families in this country grapple with every day. But these are quite separate matters. The referendum on 22nd May is about something else.

Simply stated, it's about supporting equality for all. That's why I'm convinced that voting Yes is the fair and the right thing to do.

"The purposes of this secular government are increasingly incompatible with the Christian view of man, or any notion of virtue that our founders would have recognized."

Catholic Institutions Should Not Be Forced to Hire Gay People

John Zmirak

In the following viewpoint, John Zmirak argues that Catholic organizations should not be mandated by law to hire gay individuals. Doing so would violate the institutions' religious and moral principles, he writes, and the United States federal government has no place forcing such organizations to accept gay people into their employ. Zmirak also claims that any Catholic charity or similar institution that refuses to hire gay people will lose its federal funding and therefore be unable to continue providing religious guidance to those in need. John Zmirak is a political commentator and the coauthor of the book The Race to Save Our Century: Five Core Principles to Promote Peace, Freedom, and a Culture of Life.

As you read, consider the following questions:

1. In lieu of federal money, to what financial alternative does Zmirak say Catholic groups will have to turn to continue servicing their communities?

2. What aspect of Catholic social teaching does Zmirak say Pope Pius XI supported in opposition to fascism and communism?

3. What does Zmirak say are the ways in which Christians can be true to their faith?

Satan is brilliant at tactics. He breezes to short-term victories that make him appear invincible. But for every Pearl Harbor he inflicts on the church, there is a longer, deeper, countermove that guarantees his defeat. That's how I'm reading the latest attempt by the [Barack] Obama administration to force Christian churches to accept homosexual behavior as normal and good.

Obama has ignored the pleas of even his pals on the "religious left"—those who were willing to collaborate with the most pro-abortion president in history—and refused to exempt their churches from his latest diktat: an executive order that denies federal contracts to any group that's unwilling to hire openly gay employees. With the stroke of a pen, like Louis XIV's decision to persecute the Huguenots, Obama has put the entire force of the $3.77 trillion federal budget behind the effort of cultural elites to impose their secular mores on the whole American people, using their own tax money against them.

You can learn more about the ever-more-ambitious, progay agenda, which will entail the persecution of churches if it's not stopped, in Robert Reilly's latest courageous book, *Making Gay Okay: How Rationalizing Homosexual Behavior Is Changing Everything*—a book so truthful and important that almost no one has the nerve to review it. Go buy it today. In ten years, such books might be illegal.

What Will Result

The short-term impact of this on faithful Christians will certainly be unpleasant. Let's assume that the leaders of the major Christian communions (Catholic, Orthodox and Evangelical) stand on principle. Churches and charities that won't collaborate will lose billions of dollars in federal funds that they had previously dispensed, channeling taxpayer money to serve the poor, recent immigrants, and others eligible for federal poverty aid. Groups such as Catholic Charities, some bishops' migration offices, and others will see their budgets slashed. They will have to scale back their services, as the needy whom they had served get their needs met somewhere else—by church groups which decide to play Judas, or outright secular agencies. The Christian groups that had relied on federal money to carry out their missions will have to look to their own church members for more donations, or their impact and clout will diminish.

There is no prospect of people going hungry, or being deported unjustly; the federal money that has been allocated to serve the poor will still be out there—but it will be sluiced through different channels. Any given church that holds fast to traditional teaching, if it wants to feed the poor or engage in community organizing, will have to use its own (tax exempt) money to do so.

Groups like Catholic Charities will have to draw closer to the church and look to the laity for donations. The laity, in turn, will have to step up, giving as they never have before.

Would that be the worst thing in the world? As I read the church's teaching on subsidiarity, any given problem ought first to be addressed by individuals and families, then private groups such as churches, and only if it cannot be solved that way referred to the government—the local government. If the locals fail to solve it, then the state government ought to get involved. Only problems that literally cannot be solved by local governments should be referred to Uncle Sam.

Religion vs. Government

That crucial piece of Catholic social teaching, which [Pope] Pius XI unfurled like a battle flag in the face of fascist and communist tyrannies, is flouted when the federal government becomes the first resort for every needy person. It's corrupted when the units of civil society such as the churches become just one more interest group feeding from the government trough. Critics of bishops' statements on immigration have had a field day with the fact that Catholic agencies receive tens of millions of dollars from the federal government for their immigration ministries—questioning whether this gives clerics a direct financial incentive to increase the number of migrants to America.

Can a Christian organization really stay true to its mission when it depends for much of its funding on a government whose morality can hardly be distinguished from that of Kermit Gosnell [a Pennsylvania doctor convicted to life imprisonment in 2013 for murdering three infants that survived abortion attempts]? Isn't it much more likely that the lure of government money will serve as a constant force to secularize that mission?

Christopher Hitchens [the late British American journalist and author] was appalled that Mother Teresa took money from Baby Doc Duvalier [the late dictator of Haiti who ruled from 1971 to 1986]. But at least it came without strings; Duvalier's thugs weren't supervising the Missionaries of Charity, making sure that all their ministries served his government's agenda. But that is precisely what happens to a religious agency that takes on a government contract. Every dollar of government money must (rightly) be spent on secular purposes.

As we see with Obama's latest order, the purposes of this secular government are increasingly incompatible with the Christian view of man, or any notion of virtue that our founders would have recognized. As I wrote in a piece on the bruited Black Mass at Harvard:

> Our country has gradually shifted from an intolerant (ca. 1688) to a tolerant (ca. 1783) Protestant culture, to a broadly religious humanism (ca. 1945), to embrace after 1968 a new and crasser creed. The lowest common denominator on which we can all agree boils down to this: Suffering is worse than being happy, and being alive is better than being dead—except if it means that you will suffer.
>
> That is the sum total of what Americans can agree on, the fighting creed of the free world for which we expect our soldiers to march off and die. The triumph of this new religion is everywhere apparent, and it's the only rational way to explain to your grandmother how it is that gay marriage is now legal in most places where cigarette smoking isn't, and why states that shrug at sadistic pornography grimly insist upon seat belts.
>
> The God of the Happy Moments is a jealous god, and his zealots are proving to be bigots.

Secular liberals are no longer willing to collaborate with the churches on humanitarian missions, and agree to disagree about the rest. This widely applauded executive order makes that perfectly clear: Liberals are now openly intolerant of orthodox Christianity, and they plan to keep on tightening the screws.

A New Opportunity

We can only be true to our faith when we use our own time and talents, when we spend our own money, to promote the distinctly Christian vision of human flourishing—which is increasingly incompatible with what liberals consider "decent."

So by cutting the spigot of federal money to church-based agencies, Obama has done us a paradoxical favor—as [Giuseppe] Garibaldi [a nineteenth-century Italian general and politician] unwittingly aided the church by stealing the Papal States. (Would we really want them back?) However wicked are Obama's manifest intentions, he is offering us a profound opportunity to rebuild our outreach to the needy along truly Christian lines. We won't be rubbing shoulders with (and taking orders from) abortionists and euthanasia doctors, or competing for grants with staffers from Planned Parenthood who teach bondage classes to teenagers. We will have to act like our ancestors in the faith, who cobbled together their pennies to build the Catholic school system and cathedrals like St. Patrick's.

> "Bishops fully intend to continue their efforts to uphold discrimination against LGBT people in church and society, even as their flock grows increasingly angry at this position."

Catholic Leadership Should Stop Discriminating Against Gay People

Taboola

In the following viewpoint, Taboola contends that contrary to widespread belief, many Catholics actually support both gay rights and gay marriage. Taboola claims the confusion ensues from bishops and other church leaders taking hard-line stances against gay rights and misrepresenting the modern, inclusive views of everyday Catholics. The only way for Catholics to shatter their church's veneer of discrimination toward gay people, Taboola argues, is to take active roles in personally inviting the gay community to share in the Catholic faith. Taboola is a global content-discovery company that distributes published works across the Internet to interested third parties.

As you read, consider the following questions:

1. What does Taboola say were the results of a March 2011 study by the Public Religion Research Institute?

2. What does Taboola say the US Conference of Catholic Bishops, under the direction of Cardinal Timothy Dolan, directed all American Catholic dioceses to do?

3. What are some ways Taboola suggests Catholics can help gay people in their faith communities?

A new Pew Research Center study provides an abysmal assessment of the Catholic Church for those of us who value LGBT [lesbian, gay, bisexual, and transgender] inclusion in our faith communities. In a study of 1,197 LGBT adults released on June 13, 2013, 79 percent of those questioned rated Catholicism as "unfriendly" to LGBT people. Only 4 percent view our church as "friendly."

This is probably not surprising to many, due to the long list of anti-LGBT statements, actions and positions promoted by leaders of the Catholic Church, both here in the U.S. and across the globe in recent decades. Even as the study was being released, word of Pope Francis's acknowledgement of a "gay lobby" within the Vatican and his linkage of that phrase with corruption among church leaders raised anxiety among LGBT Catholics. We wonder what it is we'll be blamed for this time, even as media representatives and others scramble to interpret what the pope meant in his speech.

Differences of Opinion

However, for those of us who identify as Catholic and LGBT, as supportive family members, or simply as ordinary Catholics dismayed by the Pew survey's findings, it raises at least two key challenges. First, it forces us to question how these numbers can coexist with other national surveys that repeatedly demonstrate that U.S. Catholics support civil rights for LGBT people at levels higher than any other denomination, and that relatively few Catholics view same-sex relationships as sinful. For example, in a March 2011 study by Public Religion Research Institute, 71 percent of Catholics supported civil marriage for same-sex couples, and only 39 percent said homosexual behavior was morally wrong.

We've also seen a succession of high-ranking Catholic public officials, including Vice President [Joe] Biden; Govs. [Andrew] Cuomo, [Christine] Gregoire, [Martin] O'Malley, and [Pat] Quinn (all former except Cuomo); and a host of congressional and state legislative leaders speak out about how their faith has led them to support or even lead efforts to further LGBT equality. Catholics increasingly cite their social justice commitments in letters to the editor and other statements supportive of same-sex marriage. Clearly, while Catholics in general are supportive of LGBT people, the church is still perceived as unwelcoming. This seems to indicate that the church is so identified with the positions assumed by its leadership that the reality of support among "rank-and-file" Catholics is rendered essentially meaningless, at least in the religious context.

In addition, we are challenged to revisit episodes like Cardinal Timothy Dolan's Easter statements that the church needs to be more welcoming to lesbian and gay people. Since his statements to that effect on two national television news shows, the cardinal has failed to respond to invitations from several groups of Catholics involved in ministry with LGBT Catholics and our families to talk about what a more welcoming church might look like.

The Church's Brand Crisis

The U.S. Conference of Catholic Bishops, which Cardinal Dolan currently serves as president, recently sent bulletin announcements and preaching points to all the Catholic dioceses across the country, directing them how to use the recent feast of Trinity Sunday to denounce marriage equality. A small group of people attempting to bring attention to the cardinal's blog saying gay people are welcome at the table but must first wash our hands were prohibited by police from entering St. Patrick's Cathedral. A bishop on Long Island under Dolan's supervision who had removed a gay man from volunteer ministry—after receiving an anonymous letter complaining that this parishioner had legally married another man—returned 18,000 petitions demanding reinstatement with a brusque, dismissive note.

In essence, Cardinal Dolan, and by extension Catholic leaders across the U.S., may have briefly benefited from some great sound bites but then failed to do anything substantive to improve the real situation of LGBT people and our families. In fact, the Trinity Sunday campaign indicates that the bishops fully intend to continue their efforts to uphold discrimination against LGBT people in church and society, even as their flock grows increasingly angry at this position.

The Pew survey should serve as a wake-up call to Catholics—not only those supportive of LGBT equality but all those who in conscience disagree with the bishops on a broad range of issues related to gender and sexuality, from women's ordination to birth control. We need to grapple with the fact that our bishops are defining Catholicism in a way that is directly opposed to what most Catholics believe and want our church to be. We have a worse brand-identity issue than JCPenney!

If we want Catholicism to be identified as a hostile institution by four out of five LGBT people, and by many of those who support us, then let the bishops continue to own "Catholic, Inc." However, if we truly believe in the baptismal identity we reaffirm each Easter season and want our church to be seen as a help and haven for those in need, it is time for Catholics to claim a leadership role within our church, much as we have done in the public square. We must begin to take on the bishops when they act in ways that are contrary to our

Ministering to Gay Individuals

- Persons who experience same-sex attraction and yet are living in accord with church teaching should be encouraged to take an active role in the life of the faith community. However, the church has a right to deny roles of service to those whose behavior violates her teaching. . . .

- For some persons, revealing their homosexual tendencies to certain close friends, family members, a spiritual director, confessor, or members of a church support group may provide some spiritual and emotional help and aid them in their growth in the Christian life. In the context of parish life, however, general public self-disclosures are not helpful and should not be encouraged.

- Sad to say, there are many persons with a homosexual inclination who feel alienated from the church. Outreach programs and evangelization efforts ought to be mindful of such persons. In areas where there are larger concentrations of homosexual persons, individuals may profitably be dedicated solely to outreach ministry to them; in other areas, ministry to persons with a homosexual inclination should be included as part of overall evangelization efforts.

- Church policies should explicitly reject unjust discrimination and harassment of any persons, including those with a homosexual inclination. . . .

*"Ministry to Persons with a Homosexual Inclination:
Guidelines for Pastoral Care," United States Conference
of Catholic Bishops, November 14, 2006.*

central creed that God is incarnate in all humans, including LGBT people and those who love and support us.

Catholics Can Help

There are many options for Catholics troubled by the findings of the recent Pew survey. Most effective would be ensuring that anytime a church leader says something untrue, unkind or unwarranted about LGBT people; fires someone due to sexual orientation, gender identity, marital status, or an expression of support for LGBT people; or takes a position on a public matter that upholds institutional discrimination, call him out on it. Let him and others know that he is speaking only for a minority of Catholics.

If you know LGBT people in your parish or faith community, tell them you're glad for their presence and gifts. Ask if they find the community supportive, or if they find anything that happens there discomforting. If a priest delivers an anti-gay message, let him know you find it problematic, given Jesus's model of broad inclusion.

I hope the Pew research is repeated, and that action among the members of our faith will lead to a better result in the next report.

| "The simple fact is that those who are dominated by same-sex attraction have no place in the priesthood."

Should the Catholic Church Ordain Gay Priests?

Michael Brown

In the following viewpoint, Michael Brown argues that the Catholic Church should not ordain gay men as priests. He claims that this should not be viewed as discrimination but rather as a practicality. Brown believes that gay priests who live together in seminaries will eventually succumb to sexual temptation and that this is unacceptable behavior in the Catholic Church. To remove the threat of what he sees as sexual deviancy from the church, Brown argues that gay men should be barred from the priesthood. Brown hosts the nationally syndicated radio talk show The Line of Fire. *He is the author of* The Real Kosher Jesus: Revealing the Mysteries of the Hidden Messiah.

As you read, consider the following questions:

1. What does Brown's source cite as a critical factor in the Catholic Church's decision to bar gay men from the priesthood?

2. What does Brown say is the difference between "same-sex attracted" Christians and "gay Christians"?

3. What other sexual danger does Brown believe gay priests could pose later in their ministries?

The recent comments of Pope Francis have created a media feeding frenzy.

What exactly did he mean when he said he would not judge gay priests? Is he now condoning homosexuality?

And is he softening the stance of his predecessor, Pope Benedict, who wrote that men with deep-seated homosexual tendencies should not serve in the priesthood? (Wait a second. Does anyone really think it's wise for a man with deep-seated homosexual tendencies to make a lifetime vow of celibacy and serve side by side with other men of like inclination? We'll come back to that question in a moment.)

During a media interview while returning from Rio to Rome, the pope was asked about the gay lobby in the Vatican. He responded, "There's a lot of talk about the gay lobby, but I've never seen it on the Vatican ID card!"

He continued, "When I meet a gay person, I have to distinguish between their being gay and being part of a lobby. If they accept the Lord and have goodwill, who am I to judge them? They shouldn't be marginalized. The tendency [to homosexuality] is not the problem. . . . They're our brothers."

What exactly did Pope Francis mean? According to John-Henry Westen (https://www.lifesitenews.com/news/what-pope-francis-could-not-mean-regarding-gay-priests-and-what-he-actually), writing on LifeSiteNews.com, we must interpret the pope's comments in the context of the historic, foundational teaching of the Catholic Church.

Westen notes, "The Catholic faith teaches that all homosexual acts are presented in Sacred Scriptures as 'acts of grave depravity'; that they are 'intrinsically disordered' and that 'under no circumstances can they be approved.' (Catechism 2357)"

The Catechism also teaches that "even the homosexual inclination is 'objectively disordered' and is a 'trial' for most who experience it. (Catechism 2358)"

At the same time, "They must be accepted with respect, compassion and sensitivity. Every sign of unjust discrimination in their regard should be avoided. (Catechism 2358)"

So, is it possible that Francis was simply restating standard Catholic doctrine—namely, that one shouldn't be judged for having same-sex attractions, as long as those attractions are not acted upon, in obedience to God? Was that his point, but stated with an emphasis on compassion, in keeping with his character?

That is certainly possible, especially in light of the clear statement on marriage made jointly by Francis and Benedict less than one month ago. As reported in the gay press (http://www.advocate.com/politics/religion/2013/07/05/popes-francis-benedict-jointly-condemn-same-sex-marriage), "Popes Francis, Benedict Jointly Condemn Same-Sex Marriage."

In fact, according to a Spanish language publication (http://lastdaywatchman.blogspot.com/2013/07/the-imminent-abortion-legalization-in.html), when the pope was asked by another journalist why he didn't speak out against abortion and same-sex marriage on his trip to Brazil, he responded, "The Church has clearly spoken about that; it is not necessary to go over it again, as it's not necessary to talk about fraud, lying or other things about which the church has a clear doctrine. It is not necessary to talk about that, but about positive things that open the road for the young ones. Besides, young people know perfectly well what is the church's position about this."

How interesting that the media has failed to pick up on this quote!

Difficulty of Gay Priests

While homosexuals may take heart from the call for acceptance, it is nevertheless difficult for homosexuals relying solely on Vatican documents and the language of the church's moral theology to accept their sexuality, an integral part of any human person as a positive aspect of their personality.

For the homosexual priest, a man called to communicate the love of God to others, this can prove especially problematic. Experiencing acceptance from God for one's created self is an important step in the spiritual life of any Christian. Two challenges follow. First, the difficulty for a priest striving to communicate acceptance and love from the church when a constitutive part of his personality is labelled by the church as objectively disordered. Second, the difficulty of carrying out the church's work, particularly his sacramental ministry, while knowing that the church considers him ordered toward an intrinsic moral evil.

There is also the related inability to draw publicly on one's own personal experience in homilies, counseling or any other type of pastoral work, as the heterosexual priest can easily do. Many heterosexual priests, for example, often speak movingly about giving up a life with a wife and children. Likewise, many priests who are recovering alcoholics speak about the liberating recovery process as a profound spiritual gift. The first challenge, therefore, is balancing church teaching with the acceptance of one's entire self as created and loved by God.

James Martin,
"The Church and the Homosexual Priest,"
America, *November 4, 2000.*

What about the issue of gay priests?

According to Westen, "Especially after the horrors of the sex abuse crisis, which many have seen to be related to past tolerance of an active gay subculture within the church, the Catholic Church has forbidden even those men with fixed homosexual inclinations from entering the seminary. In November 2005, the Congregation for Catholic Education released the 'Instruction Concerning the Criteria for the Discernment of Vocation with Regard to Persons with Homosexual Tendencies in View of Their Admission to the Seminary and to Holy Orders.'

"The Instruction forbade admission to seminary to 'those who practise homosexuality, present deep-seated homosexual tendencies or support the so-called "gay culture."'"

Obviously, men like this are not suitable candidates for the priesthood, and it's hard to believe Pope Francis would now be reversing this policy.

This is not a matter of bigotry toward gays. It's a matter of common sense.

Responding to the pope's comments, Cardinal Timothy Dolan stated (http://billmuehlenberg.com/2013/07/30/three-church-leaders-on-homosexuality/) that a priest's homosexuality "wouldn't matter to me as long as one is leading a virtuous and chaste life." But he also noted there was a potential problem in speaking of gay priests or the like, explaining, "My worry is that we're buying into the vocabulary that one's person is one's sexual identity, and I don't buy that, and neither does the church."

To be sure, there are plenty of Christian men who have not experienced change in their same-sex attractions but who have chosen to be celibate, and they are living satisfied, full lives, identifying as Christians who are same-sex attracted rather than as "gay Christians." (I think of Christopher Yuan, coauthor with his mother, Angela, of the moving book *Out of a Far Country*.)

But that is very different than ordaining into the priesthood men who are struggling with same-sex attraction, thereby putting them all together in the same environment. This would be like heterosexual priests sharing living quarters with heterosexual nuns. How long do you think their vows of celibacy would last?

In the same way, do we really think that a bunch of young gay men living together in a seminary setting will all be saintly enough to keep themselves pure? And is it realistic to think that, later in their ministries, they will not struggle as they work alone with their teenage altar boys? (These are the very environments that celibate, same-sex attracted Christians would avoid.)

And if it was right to condemn the sex scandals that have taken place in the Catholic Church, how can the church be criticized for refusing to ordain priests with deep-seated homosexual tendencies? (On a side note, in one of the most blatant examples of sticking one's head in the sand, many gay activists have denied that these sexual abuse scandals had anything to do with homosexuality.)

The simple fact is that those who are dominated by same-sex attraction have no place in the priesthood, and compassion would not put someone in a place of so much temptation, nor would wisdom allow them to be placed in a position of authority where they could hurt others along with themselves.

Any change in this position is a recipe for disaster.

| *"The gay priest gives his life as fully to the church as a straight priest does."*

The Catholic Church Should Not Discriminate Against Gay Priests

James Martin

In the following viewpoint, James Martin argues that the Catholic Church is wrong to suppress the existence of gay men in its priesthood. Gay priests, Martin says, should not be ostracized but rather encouraged to contribute their spiritual gifts to the church. In Martin's view, the Catholic Church would do well not to continue discriminating against members of its own priesthood and should instead treat all priests equally, fairly, and compassionately. Martin is a Jesuit priest and semi-regular contributor to the Catholic magazine America.

As you read, consider the following questions:

1. What does Martin say the relationship has been between gay men entering the priesthood and the number of sexual abuse cases in the Catholic Church?

2. What negative consequence does Martin say results from barring gay men from the priesthood?

3. What metaphorical terms does Martin suggest using in place of marriage imagery to describe the roles of priests in the Catholic Church?

Today's [May 31, 2010] front-page story in the *New York Times*, "Prospective Catholic Priests Face Sexuality Hurdles," by Paul Vitello, about the exclusion and weeding out of gay men from seminaries and religious formation houses, made for depressing reading. Why depressing? Several reasons.

First, the article laid bare the cognitive dissonance that theatens a church that relies on celibate gay priests to carry out much of its ministerial work, and yet sets into place policies which would bar those same kinds of men from future ministry. One of Vitello's sources, Mark D. Jordan, the R.R. Niebuhr professor at Harvard Divinity School, "who has studied homosexuality in the Catholic priesthood," and has also written extensively on it, called it an "irony" that "these new regulations are being enforced in many cases by seminary directors who are themselves gay." Yes, irony.

Second is the notion that the sexual abuse crisis was primarily a question of gays in the priesthood. For one thing, the conflation of homosexuality with pedophilia has been disproven by almost every psychiatrist and psychologist. The studies are too numerous to mention. It was rebutted even by the U.S. bishops' own study. ("At this point, we do not find a connection between homosexual identity and the increased likelihood of subsequent abuse from the data that we have right now," said Margaret Smith of the John Jay College of Criminal Justice.) For another, the increasing number of gay priests entering ministry in the past few years, which critics point to as a stain on the priesthood, coincides with a diminution of sexual abuse cases in recent years. For another, the reason that you don't see any public models of healthy, mature, celibate gay priests to counteract the stereotype of the pedophile gay priest, is that they are forbidden to speak out publicly. Or they are simply afraid.

Difficulties for Gay Priests

And why wouldn't they be? Vitello provides some context.

"It is impossible for them to come forward in this atmosphere," said Marianne Duddy-Burke, the executive director of DignityUSA, an advocacy group for gay, lesbian, bisexual and transgender Catholics. "The bishops have scapegoated gay priests because gays are still an acceptable scapegoat in this society, particularly among weekly churchgoers."

Of course it is impossible—or close to impossible—for them to come forward, particularly in dioceses where bishops have spoken out against them, and have said that they will no longer [accept] their kind as priests. What priest in Brooklyn (the focus of Vitello's story) who is celibate and gay is going to want to be honest about himself now? Particularly after this quote:

> "We have no gay men in our seminary at this time," said Dr. Robert Palumbo, a psychologist who has screened seminary candidates at the diocese's Cathedral Seminary [House of Formation] in Douglaston, Queens, for 10 years. "I'm pretty sure of it." Whether that reflects rigorous vetting or the reluctance of gay men to apply, he could not say. "I'm just reporting what is," he said.

That brings us to a third depressing point, about "what is." Psychologist[s] in particular know how arduously that closeted gay men work at "passing" as straight men, often out of a deep-seated shame. Some spend their whole lives doing it. The goal of a zero-homosexual policy in seminaries, and the weeding out of gay seminarians, is bound to lead not to a climate of transparency and honesty, but to a culture of secrecy, dishonesty and hiddenness—which is one of the main things that led to the cover-up of sexual abuse. It is one of the very things that everyone—conservative and liberal—agrees needed to be changed.

In other words, an inquisitorial approach will make it far less likely that a man might feel comfortable talking about his sexuality (straight or gay) to his superiors or formators. Several seminarians, and prospective seminarians, have written to me over the past few months describing their reluctance in mentioning any aspect of their sexuality to superiors for that reason. All sexuality, psychologists say, is on a spectrum: No one is "purely" straight or gay. So what happens when a straight seminarian discovers that he has some homosexual feelings? Will he bring his questions to a superior in a seminary where gays are excluded? Will he be encouraged to speak honestly, perhaps to a psychologist or counselor, so as to move toward greater integration and freedom? This is the kind of psychologically unhealthy, terror-driven, pressure-cooker environment that I thought everyone was against.

Gay Priests Can Fulfill Their Duties

Fourth [is] the collision of the *Catechism of the Catholic Church* and current thinking. Here's what the *Catechism* says:

> Homosexual persons are called to chastity. By the virtues of self-mastery that teach them inner freedom, at times by the support of disinterested friendship, by prayer and sacramental grace, they can and should gradually and resolutely approach Christian perfection.

Apparently, some seminary directors believe that gay men cannot be chaste, or that they are more likely to be pedophiles. But that goes against the *Catechism*, which recommends chastity for gays and lesbians. So either you think that the *Catechism* is correct, and gays can be chaste. Or you think the *Catechism* is wrong; and they cannot be. The *Catechism* also states that gays and lesbians can "approach Christian perfection" through chastity. "Christian perfection" would obviously exclude sexual abuse. If that is the case, then [why] not allow them into seminaries and religious orders?

In contrast to those who believe gays are completely unfit for the priesthood and religious life, Msgr. Stephen Rossetti, a respected priest, psychologist and author, provides a measured and sensible approach to the question, which is, in my experience, somewhat more along the lines of what most dioceses and religious orders are doing these days.

Msgr. Stephen Rossetti, a psychologist at Catholic University who has screened seminarians and once headed a treatment center for abusive priests, said the screening could be "very intrusive." But he added, "We are looking for two basic qualities: the absence of pathology and the presence of health."

Msgr. Rossetti is not alone in his sensible approach. Archbishop Timothy Dolan of New York told Catholic News Service in 2005 that he felt that a man who was homosexual and could fulfill all the Vatican requirements for a healthy emotional life "shouldn't be discouraged" from entering a seminary. Other bishops and religious superiors feel the same. As Rossetti suggested, they are looking for emotionally mature Catholic men who can live chastely and celibately, straight or gay. I wish Vitello, who is a fine religion-beat reporter and wrote a generally well-reported piece, had spent more time scouting around in other dioceses, even the New York archdiocese, for a fuller picture of how seminaries and religious orders are handling this issue. On the other hand, as Vitello seemed to imply in his piece, it was hard to get anyone to talk.

And how depressing that is. In this time where "transparency" is seen as an essential value for a healthy church, we still cannot talk about this issue.

[Fifth is] the admission—in 2010—that some people are still confused by these issues of sexual orientation. "Some seminary directors were baffled by the word 'orientation,'" said

Thomas G. Plante, a psychologist and the director of the Spirituality and Health Institute at Santa Clara University, who screens seminary candidates for several dioceses in California and nationwide. Baffled by the word "orientation"? We are in trouble if "some seminary directors" don't know what "orientation" means. Perhaps Plante simply meant that they were baffled by what the Vatican meant. Either way, we are in trouble.

Gay Priests Give of Themselves

But perhaps the most depressing thing about this article was the final quote, the "outro" as journalists say, from the vocation director of the Brooklyn diocese, in which he, on the one hand, admits that homosexuals have been good priests, but, on the other hand, says that they cannot be.

The Rev. Kevin J. Sweeney, whose incoming classes of three to five seminarians each year make him one of the more successful vocation directors in the country. Half of the nation's seminaries have one or two new arrivals each a year, and one-quarter get none, according to a recent church study. Father Sweeney said the new rules were not the order of battle for a witch hunt. "We do not say that homosexuals are bad people," he said. "And sure, homosexuals have been good priests." "But it has to do with our view of marriage," he said. "A priest can only give his life to the church in the sense that a man gives his life to a female spouse. A homosexual man cannot have the same relationship. It's not about condemning anybody. It's about our world view."

Using the metaphor of marriage to the church to bar gays from orders is unhelpful. Is the only way to look a priestly vocation by comparing it to marriage? There are many other metaphors that one can use. You could suggest that the priest is the "servant leader," which doesn't imply any sort of marriage image. Or the "minister of the Word," which also doesn't imply a marital image. Or you could simply turn to the traditional image of the priest as the one who tries to be the *alter Christus*, the "other Christ." And, by the way, he wasn't married either.

A homosexual cannot, according to church teaching, have the same relationship that a straight man can. That is true. But the gay priest gives his life as fully to the church as a straight priest does. What's more, he gives up something that a straight priest does not: He gives up his dignity. He willingly makes that sacrifice, which a straight priest does not make. For unlike the straight priest, the gay priest serves a church that will not admit his existence, is trying to weed out future men like him serving, and, in general, increasingly treats his kind like a pariah.

Periodical and Internet Sources Bibliography

The following articles have been selected to supplement the diverse views presented in this chapter.

Peter Allen	"Catholic Church Is Accused of Blocking the Appointment of the First Ever Gay Ambassador to Vatican City," *Daily Mail*, April 10, 2015.
Robert P. George	"Has the Catholic Church Changed Its Teaching on Gay Marriage?," *Christian Post*, October 15, 2014.
Gary Gutting	"Unraveling the Church Ban on Gay Sex," *New York Times*, March 12, 2015.
Eric J. Layman	"Catholic Bishops Show New Tolerance Toward Gays," *USA Today*, October 13, 2014.
Michael Lipka	"Young U.S. Catholics Overwhelmingly Accepting of Homosexuality," Pew Research Center, October 16, 2014.
David Marr	"Pope's Fine Words on Homosexuality Are Useless While the Catholic Church Still Calls It a Sin," *Guardian*, October 23, 2014.
Sean Piccoli	"Catholic Gay Rights Advocate: Church Divided Over LGBT Issues," Newsmax, April 2, 2015.
Thomas Reese	"How the Bishops Should Respond to Same-Sex Marriage Decision," *National Catholic Reporter*, July 2, 2015.
Frank Schaeffer	"Here's How the Roman Catholic Condemnation of Homosexuality Can and Must Change," Patheos, March 12, 2015.

OPPOSING
VIEWPOINTS®
SERIES

CHAPTER 2

What Role Does the Catholic Church Play in Health Issues?

Chapter Preface

In the mid-2010s, US president Barack Obama engendered scathing criticism from the United States Conference of Catholic Bishops (USCCB) for including certain mandatory prescriptions in the universal health care plans implemented through the Patient Protection and Affordable Care Act (PPACA). These prescriptions forced some American Catholic institutions to provide contraception for their employees, a prospect the bishops opposed as a violation of their church's long-standing pro-life position.

In 2013, in the midst of the ongoing disagreement between the bishops and the US federal government, Cardinal Timothy Dolan, the leader of the Archdiocese of New York, stated that although the USCCB firmly opposed Obama's contraception mandate, the bishops essentially agreed with him that efficient health care should be provided universally. Dolan noted that the bishops had in fact been advocating for such a law since 1919.

Dolan was referring to the National Catholic Welfare Council, a precursor to the USCCB. Beginning in 1919, this assembly of bishops began convening annually to deliberate how to integrate Catholic social justice more fully into American law. Among the matters discussed at these meetings were welfare, education, and health care. One of the bishops' most strongly held beliefs was that the federal government should provide these various forms of social justice to any and all citizens who needed them, especially the poor. To the bishops, this was the only way to respect the inherent dignity of all persons.

The National Catholic Welfare Council, later the United States Conference of Catholic Bishops, and the Catholic Church as a whole continued to support such universal health care legislation as the twentieth century continued. In his

1963 papal encyclical *Pacem in Terris* (Peace on Earth), Pope John XXIII grouped health care together with food and shelter as rights, rather than privileges, of all people. In 1991 Pope John Paul II affirmed this view in his encyclical *Centesimus Annus* (The Hundredth Year). Into the 2000s and 2010s, the American Catholic bishops still strongly advocated health care for all.

Throughout the church's ongoing support for this issue, however, Catholic leadership had maintained that it opposed any medical procedures that violated its pro-life stance and, therefore, human dignity. These included having abortions, using contraception, and allowing terminally ill patients to die before their natural death. It was the church's unwillingness to compromise on these principles that set the stage for the USCCB's dispute with the Obama administration in the mid-2010s, as the president's health care plan coerced some Catholic employers—selected through a complex series of stipulations based on finances and customer bases, among other criteria—to purchase for their employees health insurance plans that included contraceptives.

The following chapter presents numerous arguments relating to the Catholic Church and its views on certain aspects of health care. These subjects include the PPACA contraception mandate, abortion, family planning, and the morality of death with dignity laws.

"*There is a word for this classification system: discrimination. It is government choosing religious winners and losers.*"

Obamacare Discriminates Against Catholicism and Other Religions

L. Martin Nussbaum

In the following viewpoint, L. Martin Nussbaum argues that health care plans under the Patient Protection and Affordable Care Act, also known as Obamacare, unfairly discriminate against certain religious institutions by forcing some employers and not others to pay for contraception for their employees. To prove his point, Nussbaum tracks Obamacare's intricate stipulations concerning which religious groups are exempt from having to pay the coverage and which are not. Nussbaum believes the federal government has no constitutional authority to do this. Nussbaum is a First Amendment attorney in Colorado Springs, Colorado.

As you read, consider the following questions:

1. What kind of objections does Nussbaum claim ministry employers will raise over Obamacare's religious classifications?

2. What two religious groups does Nussbaum say a statute of Obamacare excuses from the individual health care mandate?

3. What examples of second-class religious employers does Nussbaum provide?

In January 2012, Kathleen Sebelius, secretary of the U.S. Dept. of Health and Human Services (HHS), ordered that health care plans include free contraceptives, abortion-inducing drugs and devices, sterilization, and related counseling (the "CASC mandate").

Because Evangelical Protestant ministries conscientiously oppose abortifacients and the Catholic Church conscientiously opposes the entire CASC mandate, an historic number of religious employers—over 200—sued the United States seeking freedom to practice what they preach. The Supreme Court has now agreed to hear two of those cases—*[Burwell v.] Hobby Lobby* and *Conestoga Wood Specialties [v. Burwell]*. Each involves a for-profit employer operating according to its owners' religious values. The issue is not whether corporations have standing to invoke the Religious Freedom Restoration Act (RFRA). Church and ministry corporations routinely receive such standing. The issue is whether corporations lose such protection when they are privately owned and profit oriented. Thirty-three of the 39 (85 percent) lower courts hold they do not.

This is the first wave of religious liberty lawsuits. The second wave—well under way—will include more nonprofit ministry employers like the Little Sisters of the Poor. As before, many will invoke RFRA. Some will also raise establishment clause objections because Obamacare includes a seldom noted system of discriminatory religious classifications.

In its 1982 *Larson v. Valente* decision, the U.S. Supreme Court said that "[t]he clearest command of the establishment clause" is that the government cannot prefer one religious group over another. It struck down a Minnesota statute that imposed a charitable solicitation registration requirement only on religious groups receiving over 50 percent of their income from non-member donors. In 2008, the Tenth Circuit similarly struck down a Colorado law that gave scholarships to college students attending "sectarian" colleges but not if the college was "pervasively sectarian."

Obamacare's New Precedent

Obamacare's religious classifications are far more extreme. It creates four classes of those religiously opposed to the CASC mandate: (1) those excused; (2) those "accommodated" if they hire surrogates to provide CASC benefits; (3) those eligible to plead for RFRA protection; and (4) those that must provide the coverage or pay fines up to $36,500 per employee annually.

The first class is created by statute and regulation. The statute excuses two religious groups from the individual mandate—Anabaptists and those in health care sharing ministries. Anabaptists include Amish, Brethren, Hutterites, Mennonites and the Bruderhof. The statute also exempts members of health care sharing ministries formed before Dec. 31, 1999. Only three Protestant groups qualify: Medi-Share, Christian Healthcare Ministries, and Samaritan Ministries. Members of identical programs formed after 1999 need not apply.

By regulation, the administration also exempts "churches," "their integrated auxiliaries," "conventions or associations of churches," and "the exclusively religious activities of any religious order." If a ministry of a church separately incorporates, it loses its exemption. An unincorporated parish social minis-

HHS Mandate Is Unlawful

In holding that the HHS [Department of Health and Human Services] mandate is unlawful, we reject HHS's argument that the owners of the companies forfeited all RFRA [Religious Freedom Restoration Act] protection when they decided to organize their businesses as corporations rather than sole proprietorships or general partnerships. The plain terms of RFRA make it perfectly clear that Congress did not discriminate in this way against men and women who wish to run their businesses as for-profit corporations in the manner required by their religious beliefs.

Since RFRA applies in these cases, we must decide whether the challenged HHS regulations substantially burden the exercise of religion, and we hold that they do. The owners of the businesses have religious objections to abortion. . . . If the owners comply with the HHS mandate, they believe they will be facilitating abortions, and if they do not comply, they will pay a very heavy price—as much as $1.3 million per day . . . in the case of one of the companies. If these consequences do not amount to a substantial burden, it is hard to see what would.

Under RFRA, a government action that imposes a substantial burden on religious exercise must serve a compelling government interest, and we assume that the HHS regulations satisfy this requirement. But in order for the HHS mandate to be sustained, it must also constitute the least restrictive means of serving that interest, and the mandate plainly fails that test.

Samuel J. Alito, majority opinion, Burwell, Secretary of Health and Human Services, et al. v. Hobby Lobby Stores, Inc., US Supreme Court, June 30, 2014.

try is exempt. An incorporated one is not, even though its work is identical. The Little Sisters of the Poor religious order is exempt. Its separately incorporated nursing homes are not, even though they are staffed and run by the Little Sisters because of their religious calling. The classification scheme also distinguishes "integrated auxiliaries" from non-integrated ones. The primary test for "integration" is that the sponsoring church provides a majority of the funds. This is the same criteria violating the establishment clause in *Larson*. Determining whether the activities of religious orders are "exclusively religious" or "partially religious" has an additional constitutional infirmity because such analysis inevitably entangles the courts in religious doctrine.

Second-class religious employers include separately incorporated ministries like schools and colleges; faith-based charities; religious hospitals; and parachurch ministries. Under Obamacare, these do not merit full exemption from the CASC mandate. Instead, they are required to enter agreements and give notices to their insurers or third party administrators obligating those contractors to provide CASC benefits to the ministries' employees. This no more alleviates their religious consciences than the Civil War draft alleviated Christian pacifists' consciences by exempting them if they hired surrogates to fight.

The lowest class of religious employers is for-profit corporations owned by religious individuals and operated with religious values. They are further subclassified. In her Tenth Circuit argument in *Hobby Lobby*, the Department of Justice attorney allowed that, if the for-profit employer was a sole proprietorship or general partnership, it had standing to invoke RFRA. But if the same business was a limited partnership or a corporation, it could not.

There is a word for this classification system: discrimination. It is government choosing religious winners and losers—a practice discredited by 1,600 years of Western history and forbidden in America as an establishment of religion.

> "Unfortunately, the anti-abortion zeal-
> otry of the Roman Catholic bishops in-
> volves scrupulosity—not intelligent,
> reasonable, responsible moral reason-
> ing."

Catholics Should Not Use Arguments Based on Moral Reasoning Against Obamacare

Thomas Farrell

In the following viewpoint, Thomas Farrell argues that justices of the US Supreme Court should not have used Catholic moral reasoning in deciding the Burwell v. Hobby Lobby *case, which granted the Hobby Lobby store chain the right to refuse to pay for its employees' contraception. Farrell contends that few people involved in the case would have been familiar with the esoteric intricacies of Catholic morality, especially when the owners of Hobby Lobby were not Catholic and the justices were representing a non-Catholic government. Farrell also fundamentally disagrees with the justices' decision, claiming that a business paying for its employees' contraception does not constitute an evil act. Farrell is professor emeritus of writing studies at the University of Minnesota Duluth.*

As you read, consider the following questions:

1. What does Farrell say is the reason the owners of Hobby Lobby objected to paying for employee health insurance that included contraception?

2. What does Farrell say is one element of a discussion of Roman Catholic teaching on cooperation with evil?

3. What kind of reasoning does Farrell believe Catholics should use in place of scrupulosity in arguing the abortion debate?

As everybody knows, the Roman Catholic bishops in the United States have stirred up an enormous amount of ill will as the result of their anti-abortion zealotry. The bishops mistakenly claim that distinctively human life begins at the moment of conception—that is, at the moment when the sperm fertilizes the egg.

So the Roman Catholic bishops object to all 20 FDA [Food and Drug Administration]–approved forms of contraception that are mandated under Obamacare [referring to the Patient Protection and Affordable Care Act]. But under Obamacare, churches have been exempted from the contraception mandate.

As everybody knows, six of the nine justices on the Supreme Court today come from a Roman Catholic background. (Disclosure: I come from a Roman Catholic background. However, for many years now, I have not been a practicing Catholic. I am theistic humanist, as distinct from a secular humanist.)

As everybody knows, in *Burwell v. Hobby Lobby*, the five male Catholic justices on the Supreme Court ruled in favor of the religious liberty of the owners of Hobby Lobby. The majority ruling held that closely held corporations such as Hobby Lobby have religious rights.

The owners of Hobby Lobby are Evangelical Protestants, not Roman Catholics. The owners objected to the contraceptive mandate in Obamacare. More specifically, the owners objected to having to pay for health insurance for their employees that would cover four specific forms of contraception, because they mistakenly believe those four forms of contraception to be abortion inducing. (The owners already pay for health insurance that covers the other 16 FDA-approved forms of contraception, all of which the Catholic bishops object to.)

So the Supreme Court ruled that the religious rights of the employers trump the rights of their employees to those four forms of contraception.

An Unusual Standard

As a result of this ruling, we Americans now are going to have both nonprofit corporations such as churches and for-profit closely held corporations such as Hobby Lobby eligible to apply for exemption to the contraception mandate in Obamacare.

But a curious thing emerges in the ruling written by Justice Samuel Alito. Leslie C. Griffin, a law professor at the University of Nevada, Las Vegas, calls attention to this in her essay "Catholic Moral Theology at the Supreme Court" that she posted at the website of the Jesuit-sponsored *America* magazine (dated July 2, 2014).

Professor Griffin points out that in footnote 34, Justice Alito cites Fr. Henry Davis's book *Moral and Pastoral Theology* (1935) as the source of certain supposedly legal reasoning in the text of the majority's ruling. The Roman Catholic Church has a long tradition of carefully worked out moral reasoning about formal and material cooperation with supposed evil.

So let us pause now and savor this. The five Roman Catholic justices on the Supreme Court of the United States have drawn on their familiarity with Roman Catholic moral reasoning to write the majority ruling in *Burwell v. Hobby Lobby*.

Principle of Cooperation in Evil

The principle of cooperation in evil has been developed in the Catholic moral tradition as a guide to assist with the identification of different types of cooperation and the conditions under which cooperation may or may not be tolerated. Moralists have long recognized that under many circumstances, it would be impossible for an individual to do good in the world, without being involved to some extent in evil. . . . One may be able to justify certain types of cooperation, but this justification ought not to be confused with an obligation to cooperate in evil acts. Justification and obligation represent two different moral categories.

"What Is the Principle of Cooperation of Evil?,"
National Catholic Bioethics Center.

In effect, the owners of Hobby Lobby were indeed objecting to their mandated cooperation with supposed evil (i.e., the four forms of contraception that their employees might freely choose to use under Obamacare).

In a fine example of an ecumenical spirit toward the Evangelical Protestant owners of Hobby Lobby, the five male Roman Catholic justices drew on their familiarity with Roman Catholic moral reasoning to write their legal ruling. No doubt the five Roman Catholic justices could claim that they were exercising their religious freedom by drawing on Catholic moral reasoning in writing their legal ruling.

I don't want to be overly subtle here. We Americans should think of the law and legal reasoning as a smaller circle within the bigger circle of moral reasoning. Moral reasoning should be more comprehensive and inclusive than the law and legal reasoning.

Off the top of my head, I cannot recite the long history of the Roman Catholic tradition of moral reasoning about formal and material cooperation with evil. However, I can tell you that the discussion involves Aristotle's ideas about form and matter—that is, formal and material cooperation are used analogously with form and matter in constituting moral (or immoral) acts.

These are the kinds of distinctions that Roman Catholic priests who are going to hear confessions should study. Yes, ordinary Roman Catholics who try to live morally upright lives should also study Catholic moral reasoning to a certain extent.

But how many non-Catholic law schools offer courses on Aristotle's ideas about form and matter—or courses on Roman Catholic moral reasoning?

Unfitting Reasoning

So is it fair to have Roman Catholic justices on the Supreme Court draw on Roman Catholic moral reasoning in adjudicating cases, when the non-Catholic government and other lawyers presenting arguments in cases probably do not know much about Roman Catholic moral reasoning?

Professor Griffin makes the following comments: "Justice [Ruth Bader] Ginsburg cogently argued in dissent [from the majority ruling] that any burden on the Greens' and Hahns' [referring to the families represented in the *Hobby Lobby* case] religion was 'too attenuated' to qualify as substantial. The employees decide whether to use contraception, and 'no individual decision by an employee and her physician . . . is in any meaningful sense her employer's decision or action.'"

Right on, Justice Ginsburg! There would be no formal or material cooperation with supposed evil for the employer to pay for the mandated health insurance that covers all 20 FDA-approved contraceptives because there is no evil involved in using any of the 20 FDA-approved forms of contraception—the Roman Catholic bishops to the contrary notwithstanding.

In Roman Catholic tradition of thought there is a term that accurately describes the kind of moral reasoning that the majority ruling uses: scrupulosity.

Unfortunately, the anti-abortion zealotry of the Roman Catholic bishops involves scrupulosity—not intelligent, reasonable, responsible moral reasoning.

| "A society that claims a 'right' to destroy innocent human life undermines all human rights."

Catholics Should View Abortion as a Moral Evil

Richard M. Doerflinger

In the following viewpoint, Richard M. Doerflinger argues that Catholic health care providers should oppose all efforts by the US federal government to discriminate against them for not providing abortions. He claims that, according to Catholic teaching, everyone possesses the right to life, and to destroy an unborn life is a violation of a basic human right. Doerflinger also contends that the US Catholic pro-life movement should urge the federal government to protect its members' religious freedom by not forcing Catholic health centers to provide abortions. Doerflinger is associate director of pro-life activities at the United States Conference of Catholic Bishops.

As you read, consider the following questions:

1. What does Doerflinger say are the drawbacks to the otherwise effective 2004 anti-abortion legislation known as the Hyde/Weldon amendment?

Richard M. Doerflinger, "Upholding a Right not to Kill," *Life Issues Forum*, April 29, 2014. Copyright © 2014 United States Conference of Catholic Bishops. All rights reserved. Reproduced with permission.

2. What kind of health organizations does Doerflinger say compose the largest network of nonprofit health care providers in the United States?

3. What does Doerflinger say is the greatest evil that a society can perpetrate against good people?

Soon Congress will consider protecting conscience rights for health care providers, especially the right not to be forced to participate in abortion.

The issue comes up in several bills introduced this year [2014]. The most ambitious of these, and the first to be considered—with votes likely the first week of May, is the No Taxpayer Funding for Abortion Act (H.R. 3). Besides permanently banning federal funding of abortion, it would forbid all federal agencies (and state and local governments receiving federal funds) to discriminate against health care providers who decline to provide, refer for or pay for abortions.

Federal conscience laws have existed since 1973, but each has drawbacks that make it less effective than it could be. Since 2004, for example, the Hyde/Weldon [Conscience Protection] Amendment to the Labor/HHS [Labor, Health and Human Services, Education, and Related Agencies] appropriations bill has forbidden governmental discrimination against pro-life health care providers. But the amendment must be renewed each year; it only covers entities funded by that particular appropriations bill; and it does not have an enforcement mechanism allowing victims of discrimination to go to court to defend their rights. H.R. 3 remedies those defects.

Catholic Connection

This issue should be of fundamental importance to Catholics, as the survival of authentic Catholic health care is at stake. Catholic hospitals make up the largest network of nonprofit health care in the nation, providing higher quality care than secular and for-profit hospitals. And this same moral commitment to the life and well-being of each person leads Catholic health care to reject all direct abortion. If it becomes illegal to practice medicine with respect for all human life, Catholic health care will die and many patients will suffer.

Catholic moral reflection also provides a deeper reason why this issue is so important. There is a logic and a hierarchy to human rights. The most basic right, the condition for all others, is the right to live. We can't enjoy any rights—the right to vote, to speak and think freely, or to worship as we please—unless we are allowed to live long enough to exercise them. Life is the foundation stone for other human rights. But the pinnacle, the roof on the house of human rights, is the right of conscience and religious freedom. Only if we have a right to seek the truth and act on it can we promote and advance all elements of human dignity, including basic human rights. Human dignity begins with life itself, and flourishes in the freedom to worship God and do His will—including His will that we protect the most vulnerable.

A society that claims a "right" to destroy innocent human life undermines all human rights. But a society that makes its members ignore their moral and religious convictions, and take part in such destruction, has leveled the entire house. In one stroke it has violated both the most basic and the most exalted human rights. It has perpetrated the greatest evil of all, by forcing good people to make themselves complicit in grave evil.

This is what the "abortion rights" movement wants—to implicate even pro-life people in destroying unborn life, so no one can denounce their agenda without implicating themselves as well. All of us will be guilty, and all will have a vested interest in justifying the evil we do. At that point, the voices that speak for the innocent victims of abortion will be silenced.

We must prevent this from happening. We can begin by urging our elected representatives to strengthen protection for the conscience rights of health care providers who respect innocent human life.

| *"Pro-choice Catholics offer an effective counter-narrative to the idea that all people of faith oppose abortion."*

Pro-Choice Catholics Play an Important Role in the Abortion Debate

Patricia Miller

In the following viewpoint, Patricia Miller argues that pro-choice Catholics are an important voice in the ongoing abortion debate in the United States. She believes the Catholic pro-choice movement that arose in the 1970s and 1980s was vital to showing the world that not all Catholics necessarily agree with the staunch pro-life position of their church leadership. In Miller's view, Catholics can and should, in some instances, support abortion as the morally correct choice to make. Miller is the author of Good Catholics: The Battle over Abortion in the Catholic Church.

As you read, consider the following questions:

1. For what accomplishment does Miller say "Pope Patricia" should be remembered?

2. What does Miller claim was the Catholic Church's position on abortion before the fetus had been "ensouled"?

3. What does Miller say the Catholic pro-choice movement empowered Catholics to begin doing?

On an unseasonably warm January day exactly one year after the Supreme Court made abortion legal, a 49-year-old woman clad in ersatz vestments made her way up the steps of St. Patrick's Cathedral. When she reached the top of the stairs, she turned and faced a crowd of supporters intermingled with curious tourists and office workers on their lunch break. As a white-and-gold cardboard miter emblazoned with a Venus symbol was lowered onto her head, Patricia McQuillan declared herself Her Holiness Pope Patricia the First.

Pope Patricia wasted no time delivering her first encyclical. "The Catholic Church's stand on abortion is only 100 years old, is strictly political and has nothing to do with religion as taught by Jesus," declared McQuillan.

The crowning of Pope Patricia was a media sensation in New York and in feminist circles, but has largely been forgotten since. But Pope Patricia should be remembered because she gave birth to one of the most overlooked but critical components of the 40-year-plus effort to keep abortion legal in the United States: the Catholic pro-choice movement.

McQuillan christened herself Pope Patricia to bring attention to a new organization of pro-choice Catholics that she founded, Catholics for a Free Choice [(CFFC), presently known as Catholics for Choice (CFC)], at a time when it was assumed that most Catholics reflected the view of their leadership and opposed legal abortion. Indeed, in the immediate aftermath of *Roe v. Wade*, the most visible opponents of abortion were Catholic and the bishops of the Catholic Church were gaining momentum as the uncontested leaders of the burgeoning effort to roll back the decision.

As a matter of fact, at the very moment McQuillan was climbing the steps of St. Patrick's, some 6,000 largely Catholic anti-abortion protestors were gathering in Washington, D.C., for the first March for Life. Demonstrators had been recruited from parishes and parochial schools all over the Northeast and bused in from as far away as Minnesota to illustrate the clout of the Catholic anti-abortion lobby. But it was the beatific Pope Patricia in her cardboard miter and feminist vestments who graced stories about the first anniversary of *Roe* in *Time* and *Newsweek* and in newspapers from New York to Germany, signaling the birth of a distinctly Catholic abortion rights movement that would go toe-to-toe with the institutional church.

A Growing Movement

McQuillan wouldn't live to see the movement she gave birth to grow beyond its infancy. She was already suffering from metastatic breast cancer when she climbed the steps of Saint Patrick's; she died the following June. But over the next decades, the movement she founded provided a critical backstop to the bishops' efforts to overturn *Roe* by trying to marshal electoral support for an abortion ban and convince Catholics that it was an article of faith that they couldn't support abortion rights.

The movement did two critical things. First, it helped excavate and publicize an alternative Catholic theology that contradicted the narrative of the hierarchy that the church had always taught—that abortion was murder and that Catholics could never support it. As McQuillan noted, the Catholic Church had held various opinions about when a fetus is "ensouled," and that for much of its history, it had considered abortion before the fetus had a soul a sin of the flesh on par with contraception, not murder. And feminist theologians like Rosemary Radford Ruether posited that the church's ban on abortion, like its ban on contraception, had more to do with how the church viewed women than with unchangeable doctrine.

Just as importantly, the movement gave voice to the significant number of faithful, pro-choice Catholics, helping to make visible Catholic support for abortion rights. When the first congressional hearings were held in March of 1974 on a constitutional amendment to ban abortion, the four main witnesses—and the only witnesses seen on the televised portion of the hearing—were Catholic cardinals, including the head of the National Conference of Catholic Bishops, who asserted that only a complete ban on abortion was acceptable to Catholics. But when the second set of hearings commenced in September, CFFC arranged for Father Joseph O'Rourke, a pro-choice Jesuit, and Jane Furlong Cahill, a Catholic feminist theologian, to testify about Catholic support for abortion rights and the deep misogyny that informed much of the Catholic teaching about women and sex.

Lasting Change

One of the movement's landmark moments came when New York Archbishop John O'Connor criticized vice-presidential candidate Geraldine Ferraro shortly before the hotly contested presidential election of 1984 for having signed a letter from CFFC that said the Catholic position on abortion wasn't monolithic. O'Connor had already suggested that voting for a pro-choice politician was incompatible with Catholic teaching. A group of Catholic theologians and activists arranged an open letter in the *New York Times*, with some 100 priests, nuns and theologians asserting that "a diversity of opinions regarding abortion exists among committed Catholics," and that "a large number of Catholic theologians hold that even direct abortion, though tragic, can sometimes be a moral choice."

The ad generated enormous controversy. It also "effectively and finally put to rest the myth that Catholics . . . share the belief of the Vatican and the U.S. bishops that abortion is to be absolutely prohibited both legally and morally," wrote then CFFC president Frances Kissling and feminist theologian Mary Hunt.

Of course, that didn't end the controversy over Catholics and abortion. Bishops would continue to say that Catholics couldn't vote for pro-choice policy makers and Catholics would continue to make up their own minds, supporting pro-choice candidates like Bill Clinton and Barack Obama. But the movement did more than create a vibrant space for pro-choice Catholics in public life. It empowered Catholics to think for themselves on abortion. Today, a majority of Catholics support abortion rights and fewer than 20 percent recognize church leaders as the final moral authority on the issue.

And pro-choice people of faith matter more than ever, as debates over reproductive rights are increasingly fused with religious rhetoric and claims of religious freedom, as evidenced by the *[Burwell v.] Hobby Lobby* case. Pro-choice Catholics offer an effective counter-narrative to the idea that all people of faith oppose abortion. As Jon O'Brien, the current head of Catholics for Choice notes, "We are pro-choice because of our faith, not despite it."

> "The Vatican has acknowledged that the evidence suggests its position on contraception is 'commonly perceived today as an intrusion in the intimate life of the couple.'"

Pope Francis's Comments on Family Planning Are Misguided

Tara Culp-Ressler

In the following viewpoint, Tara Culp-Ressler argues that the Catholic Church should not be encouraging Catholics worldwide to use natural family planning as a form of birth control, as that method is unreliable for preventing pregnancies. Culp-Ressler believes that Pope Francis's continued promotion of this method is perpetuating Catholic families producing a large number of children. Instead of following the church's conservative teachings on the subject, Culp-Ressler suggests that Catholics consider hormonal birth control as a morally acceptable form of contraception. Culp-Ressler is the health editor of ThinkProgress.

As you read, consider the following questions:

1. What does Culp-Ressler say are some of the downsides to using natural family planning?

2. What two decisions of the Catholic Church does Culp-Ressler say are reinforcing the inefficient status quo of Catholic birth rates around the world?

3. In what two regions of the world does Culp-Ressler say Catholics are more progressive on the issue of modern birth control?

Pope Francis made international headlines on Monday [January 18, 2015] by explicitly endorsing efforts to control family size, saying that Catholics don't need to breed "like rabbits." But his comments, which come in the midst of evolving attitudes toward contraception within the Catholic Church, ultimately fail to move the dial forward for women in developing nations pushing for more access to reproductive health care.

"Some think, excuse me if I use the word, that in order to be good Catholics, we have to be like rabbits—but no," the pope told journalists during a flight back from the Philippines, concluding that about three children per family is about right.

"God gives you methods to be responsible," he added, alluding to natural family planning (NFP), which is the method of non-hormonal birth control that's sanctioned by the Catholic Church. Francis recounted meeting a woman pregnant with her eighth child after she had already had seven babies via Cesarean section, criticizing her for potentially risking her life and implying that she could have used NFP.

The Unreliable Catholic Alternative

Practicing NFP involves tracking a woman's fertility—through biological markers like taking her temperature, examining her cervical mucus, or counting the days between her menstrual cycle—and then abstaining from sex on the days when she's most likely to conceive. It can also be a useful tool for women who want to get pregnant. NFP has recently gained some popularity among American women who want an alternative to hormonal contraception.

But the method also comes with some downsides. There's a lot of room for potential error, and many couples struggle to use NFP perfectly. Some women's biological markers are more difficult to track and this method won't work as well for them, no matter how careful they are. Plus, for women in abusive relationships, or simply in marriages where the power balance is tipped in favor of the man, it's not necessarily realistic to trust their partner to always abstain from sex during "off limits" days.

Those factors contribute to the fact that, according to federal researchers, NFP has about a 24 percent failure rate—which means that about one in four women who attempt to use it as their primary birth control method end up getting pregnant. For that reason, the American College of Obstetricians and Gynecologists does not recommend NFP for women exactly like the one admonished by Pope Francis: Women who could be placed in medical danger by a pregnancy.

Placing the responsibility on Catholics to avoid procreating "like rabbits," while reiterating the Catholic Church's op position to a range of artificial birth control methods that are much more effective than NFP for many women, ultimately reinforces the status quo—even though it's one that isn't working well for Catholics around the world.

Growing Opposition

That conflict is on sharp display in the Philippines, the country where Pope Francis recently spent five days. There, the birth rate has skyrocketed, partially thanks to the Catholic hierarchy's fierce opposition to hormonal contraception and dogged promotion of NFP. Women have recently started demanding access to long-lasting birth control like IUDs (intrauterine devices). And lay Catholics have increasingly

US Catholics' Desire for Change, Compared with Expectations

Percentage of Catholics who think the Catholic Church should change teachings compared with percentage who say that by 2050, the church will definitely or probably change.

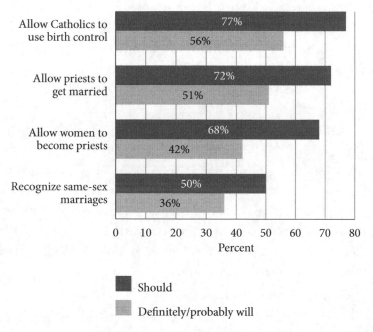

	Should	Definitely/probably will
Allow Catholics to use birth control	77%	56%
Allow priests to get married	72%	51%
Allow women to become priests	68%	42%
Recognize same-sex marriages	50%	36%

Source: Pew Research Center survey, Feb. 14–23, 2014. Based on Catholics.

TAKEN FROM: Michael Lipka, "U.S. Catholics More Hopeful than Expectant of Changes to Church Teachings," Pew Research Center, March 12, 2014.

bucked the church leadership to join those calls, advocating for greater access to birth control as a way of alleviating poverty.

Last year, the Philippine Supreme Court approved a landmark law that cleared the way for the government to give free contraception to nearly all residents, putting an end to the Roman Catholic Church's 15-year opposition campaign to state-sponsored birth control in the country. News outlets across the world reported that Filipino Catholics were "evolving" away from the church's strict teachings on reproductive health.

"We believe that you can advocate reproductive health and practice family planning, and still be a good Catholic," Bicbic Chua, the executive director of Catholics for Reproductive Health, one of the groups instrumental in advocating for the country's new law, recently told the *Wall Street Journal.* "For us what is immoral is to bring children into this world without love, proper care, and nourishment."

Similar dynamics are playing out across the world. A recent global poll of self-identified Catholics found that the vast majority of them disagree with the church's prohibition against hormonal birth control. Seventy-eight percent of Catholics across all countries surveyed said they support the use of modern birth control—a number that rises even further in European and Latin American countries, where Catholics tend to be more progressive. More than 90 percent of Catholics in France, Brazil, Spain, Argentina, and Colombia have no problem with artificial contraception.

Preliminary results from the pope's own survey of Catholics on "family issues" like birth control and divorce have returned similar findings. Catholics in Germany and Switzerland, the countries that have publicized the survey results so far, largely reject the church's conservative teachings on birth control and same-sex marriage. The Vatican has acknowledged that the evidence suggests its position on contraception is "commonly perceived today as an intrusion in the intimate life of the couple."

Here in the United States, more than 80 percent of Catholics say that hormonal birth control is morally acceptable, and they have no problem using it. According to the Guttmacher Institute, nearly 90 percent of Catholic women of reproductive age currently use artificial contraception. Meanwhile,

Guttmacher reports that just three percent of the married Catholic women in the United States rely on NFP to avoid pregnancy.

During his trip to the Philippines last week, the Pope gave an address that has been described as his "strongest defense yet" of the church's ban on birth control. Although his "rabbit" comments have largely been received well (except among rabbit breeders, of course), they actually fall along the same conservative lines.

| "The truth is, people are having too many kids, and it isn't just Catholics."

Pope Francis Is Correct to Encourage Conservative Family Planning

Tyler Anderson

In the following viewpoint, Tyler Anderson argues that Pope Francis's warning to Catholics not to have too many children is sound advice in an overpopulated world. With more than seven billion people on the planet, Anderson says, the world's natural resources are being depleted with little hope of being replaced. Anderson proposes as a solution giving all people everywhere access to free birth control to encourage responsible family planning. Anderson is a contributor at the Lantern, *the student newspaper of the Ohio State University.*

As you read, consider the following questions:

1. What does Anderson identify as some of the negative effects on society that overpopulation causes?

2. What does Anderson propose doing to slow birth rates across the world?

3. What does Anderson say results from upholding social stigmas on sex and birth control?

In light of a few words recently uttered by the great Pope Francis, I'd like to take this opportunity to write about the very serious issue of overpopulation.

While it's true that I would feel much more comfortable discussing Sunday's Screen Actors Guild Awards or Taylor Swift's recently discovered belly button, I think this is important. Besides, Pope Francis is basically Beyoncé for Catholic people, right? It's like pop culture for sheltered parochial school students.

The pope recently commented that in order to be "good Catholics," people need not feel the urge to breed "like rabbits." I give major props to the guy for tossing out that colloquial phrase, but he should've known people wouldn't be too happy about it. And being in the position of power that he is, Pope Francis had no choice but to apologize through an archbishop in a more thoughtful and family-friendly way.

But I want to speculate on his original message.

The truth is, people are having too many kids, and it isn't just Catholics. Our world has way too many people, and that fact becomes more apparent each and every day.

I'm saying it, because someone has to say it. And it's true. Our population is skyrocketing at alarming rates. Experts estimate that we've broken the 7 billion mark, and that number is quickly making its way to 8 billion. But people don't want to hear that they should stop having children. And ethically speaking, it's a limitation that even I can't justify.

But we have to do something about it.

Population Control

Food shortages, pollution, climate change and countless other problems that threaten society can be traced to the simple fact that we have too many people. We have too many people, and we do not have enough resources to support them.

Overpopulation: Environmental and Social Problems

Human population is growing like never before. We are now adding *one billion* people to the planet every 12 years. That's about 220,000 per day. . . .

Many basic resources are strained by our current population:

> Food: one billion people, one out of every seven people alive, go to bed hungry. Every day, 25,000 people die of malnutrition and hunger-related diseases. Almost 18,000 of them are children under 5 years old. Food production and distribution could catch up if our population stopped growing and dropped to a sustainable level.

> Water shortages: About one billion people lack access to sufficient water for consumption, agriculture and sanitation. Aquifers are being depleted faster than they can be replenished. Melting glaciers threaten the water supply for billions. . . .

> Air quality: Childhood asthma rates have risen dramatically in the past 20 years. The problems are not limited to the industrialized countries with their automobiles and factories. Children in undeveloped countries, where people depend on burning wood and dung for their heat and cooking, are also at risk.

> *"Overpopulation:*
> *Environmental and Social Problems,"*
> *Institute for Population Studies.*

It's easier to govern a nation of 1 million than it is a nation of 1 billion. It's easier to feed two mouths than it is to feed four, and it's easier to delete 10 Candy Crush invitations than it is to delete 20. Diversity is good, and there is strength in numbers. But at some point, a community suffers when it becomes too dense.

So how do we control our population when our very instinct seeks to promote it? Our entire society is built upon the idea of growth, and yet, in my opinion, that growth is causing the vast majority of our struggles.

We can't force people to stop having children. It simply wouldn't be fair. Instead, we need to educate. We need to spread awareness regarding the consequences of overpopulation. We need to teach people what it truly means to raise a child. We need to realize that mass-producing these wrinkly little angels—which are more or less shrieking bags of meat—will inevitably suck up all our hard-earned money.

Nobody should be told that they should not have children, but everyone should know that it's not a decision to make lightly.

In addition to education, access to birth control should be a nonissue by now. Condoms should be free and easily obtained in schools and clinics. If a woman wants to prevent her body from producing a child, then her decision should be seen as intelligent and respectable. She should not have to deal with outside forces that seek to threaten her decision.

As a society, we harbor far too many needless taboos on this subject. We uphold these arbitrary stigmas on the ethics of marriage, sex and birth control, and they only exist to hurt us. This behavior simply serves to produce unnecessary political debates, unnecessary restrictions on female rights, and unnecessary guilt over boinking one's high school sweetheart.

In a future that is threatened with so many potentially catastrophic outcomes, I think we would be better served by training and educating a limited group of forward thinkers than we would be to needlessly create more victims.

Anywho, that's all I got. Now If you'll excuse me, I desperately need to go catch up on *19 Kids and Counting*.

> "Human life is not a consumer com-
> modity to be thrown away when it is
> less than optimal."

Death with Dignity Opposes Catholic Teaching

Donald Hanson

*In the following viewpoint, Donald Hanson argues that accord-
ing to Christian teachings, all human life is sacred and should
be treated with respect. In Hanson's view, this applies to all
people, including those suffering from any sort of physical or
mental disability. Further, Hanson contends, people's bodies are
not their own, but belong to God. Therefore, he concludes, people
have no right to take their own lives, for any purpose. Hanson is
pastor of Most Holy Trinity Church in East Hampton, New
York.*

As you read, consider the following questions:

1. From what biblical writer does Hanson quote to prove
   that humans are God's possessions?

2. What does Hanson say is the current libertarian view of
   American culture?

3. What does Hanson say has made end-of-life and beginning-of-life issues more complex?

You have most likely read or heard about Brittany Maynard, a 29-year-old, newly married woman who was diagnosed with a malignant and inoperable brain cancer. She chose to end her life by a deliberate overdose of barbiturates prescribed by her doctor in Oregon, one of five states where assisted suicide is legal. She decided to make her choice public on social media and became part of a public campaign to influence acceptance of "death with dignity."

Brittany's story is a very sad one and we cannot but feel sorrow, not only for her, but for her husband and her family as well. But there are underlying values and assumptions here which need to be teased out and evaluated. Is suicide in this way really "death with dignity"? Is this an ethical decision which society should welcome and embrace? Clearly from a Catholic standpoint it is not. But why? Isn't this just the Catholic Church standing in the way of progress and compassion once again? I think not, and here is why.

Human Life Is Sacred

Life is a gift. It is infinitely precious and valuable. This is true whether we are born perfectly formed, incredibly talented and stunningly handsome, or whether we come into this world with some disability, whether physical, mental, or otherwise. We are God's creation and each of us is a miracle.

That also means that we are not our own. As St. Paul says to the Corinthians: "Do you not know that your body is a temple of the Holy Spirit within you, whom you have from God, and that you are not your own? For you have been purchased at a price. Therefore, glorify God in your body" (1 Co 6:19–20 NABre [New American Bible, Revised Edition]). And again in Romans: "For if we live, we live for the Lord, and if we die, we die for the Lord; so then, whether we live or die,

Physician-Assisted Suicide

There is passive euthanasia and active euthanasia. Active euthanasia refers to ending a person's life by active means, such as with drugs. This is typically what is meant by physician-assisted suicide. Passive euthanasia refers to allowing a person to die by withholding drugs, food, water, and other substances needed for survival. This is not technically considered physician-assisted suicide, although there are legalities covering this process when a person relies on a physician for their health and life.

"25 Surprising Physician-Assisted Suicide Statistics,"
HealthResearchFunding.org, July 13, 2014.

we are the Lord's" (Rom 14:8 NABre). That reality is something which secular culture does not understand and does not accept, yet it is a central part of our faith. It is more than just that God forbids suicide (which God does), but why God does: Because we are God's; life is God's gift. We—in all our imperfection—are an expression of God's love.

Although I feel sympathy for Brittany I also recognize that this is part of a marketing effort organized by pro-suicide groups. Be attentive! Doctors, for the most part, do not want to be a part of this. It directly contradicts their calling to be healers. Nor is this a private matter; it has immediate social effects. But our highly individualized contemporary American culture doesn't support that either. The libertarian view sees everyone as completely autonomous and given freedom not to be limited by anyone. That is not the Christian view. We belong to one another. We were made to be in community and fellowship. We are the body of Christ. The common good is a treasured part of our political and spiritual heritage. Extreme individualism is one of the poisoned pills our culture is handing out to us.

Respect for Death

End-of-life issues—as also beginning-of-life issues—have been made more complex because of technology. Ethical reflection has a hard time keeping pace with new scientific capabilities. But Christian ethics insists always on the dignity of the human person. Catholic moral teaching has always held that we are not obliged to take extraordinary means to prolong life. Important advances in palliative care (keeping terminal patients pain free) and the hospice movement have reduced the physical, psychological and spiritual pain of death and dying. Human life is not a consumer commodity to be thrown away when it is less than optimal. Death is part of life, not a taboo. Were we to think, feel, say or act as if there was no value or meaning to death, we would be abandoning Christ on the Cross. Jesus "loved his own in the world and he loved them to the end" (Jn 13:1 NABre). And that "end" was when he bowed his head on the cross and gave up his spirit.

Respect life. Pray for and visit the sick and suffering. Accompany the dying. Like Jesus, "love them till the end."

> "As a Catholic, I pray to God for the passage of the bills authorizing medical aid in dying."

Catholics Should Not Oppose Death with Dignity

Robert Olvera

In the following viewpoint, Robert Olvera argues that Catholics should support medical aid in dying for terminally ill patients. Doing so would show true compassion for those who are suffering with no possibility of recovery, he says. Additionally, Olvera claims, history shows no record of abuse or foul play concerning this medical aid, implying that the process is generally treated responsibly by patients and doctors. Olvera is a family physician in Orange County, California.

As you read, consider the following questions:

1. What fraction of Oregon patients does Olvera say have qualified for aid-in-dying medication but have never taken it?

2. What two similar processes does Olvera differentiate from aid in dying?

3. By what percentage margin does Olvera say seventeen thousand US doctors support patients' decisions to use medical aid in dying?

Inspired by the public advocacy of terminal brain cancer patient Brittany Maynard, lawmakers in Washington, DC, and at least 16 other states—from California to New York—have introduced bills that would authorize the medical option of aid in dying.

This legislation would allow mentally competent, terminally ill adults in the final stages of their disease the option to request a doctor's prescription for aid-in-dying medication that they could choose to take if their suffering becomes unbearable.

As a Catholic and a physician, I feel compelled to dispel the myths about these bills perpetrated by the Roman Catholic Church, some disability groups, and the American Medical Association (AMA).

Aid-in-Dying Misconceptions

The Oregon law that is the model for this legislation has a stellar 17-year track record, with no scientifically documented cases of abuse or coercion. Dying adults who go through the lengthy process of obtaining the medication in Oregon hold onto it for weeks or months, as Brittany did, before taking it, if they take it at all.

In fact, more than one-third of those who qualify for the medication never take it, according to the Oregon Public Health [Division]. But having it in their possession gives these dying patients great comfort knowing they have it if their suffering does become unbearable and there is no other medical option available to help them.

Contrary to opponents' claims, medical aid in dying is not "euthanasia." It requires a doctor or nurse—not the patient—to administer the medication. Euthanasia is illegal throughout the United States.

Aid in dying also is not "assisted suicide," as critics wrongly call it.

Widespread Support

The nation's largest public health association, the American Public Health Association (not the American Medical Association), supports aid in dying. It recognizes that "the term 'suicide' or 'assisted suicide' is inappropriate when discussing the choice of a mentally competent, terminally ill patient to seek medications that he or she could consume to bring about a peaceful and dignified death."

The five states that authorize medical aid in dying—Oregon, Washington, Montana, Vermont and New Mexico [decision overruled in 2015, making physician-assisted suicide illegal in New Mexico]—have separate laws prohibiting assisted suicide. The death certificates of terminally ill adults who utilize medical aid in dying in these states confirm that they died from their terminal disease, not assisted suicide.

In addition, 17,000 U.S. doctors from 28 medical specialties support by a 54% to 31% margin the decision of patients with "incurable and terminal" diseases who want to end their own life, according to an online survey conducted by Medscape.

Despite the opposition to medical aid in dying by some disability groups, polls of people living with disabilities show they support this end-of-life option by about the same percentage as the general population.

As physicians, we should always provide quality end-of-life care for people who are suffering from an incurable and irreversible terminal illness. Yet when a person with only months, weeks or even days to live cannot get relief from extreme pain, we should allow that person the option to end their suffering when the time comes.

My 25-year-old daughter Emily Rose desperately pleaded for this option during the final few agonizing months of her life last spring when she suffered in horrific pain from terminal leukemia, despite getting great home hospice and palliative care.

As a Catholic, I pray to God for the passage of the bills authorizing medical aid in dying. These laws would ensure that dying Americans have the option to pass peacefully in their sleep, suffer less, and spare themselves the pain of a lengthy and prolonged death that my daughter had to endure.

Periodical and Internet Sources Bibliography

The following articles have been selected to supplement the diverse views presented in this chapter.

John Bacon	"Pope Francis to Allow Priests to Forgive Abortion," *USA Today*, September 1, 2015.
Tara Culp-Ressler	"The Problem with Pope Francis Telling Catholics to Avoid Breeding 'Like Rabbits,'" *ThinkProgress*, January 20, 2015.
Joan Frawley Desmond	"Giving Death Its Due: Catholics Push Back Against Assisted-Suicide Bills," *National Catholic Register*, March 23, 2015.
Matt Hardo	"These Nuns Provide 'Death with Dignity'—but It's Not Assisted Suicide," Catholic News Agency, April 1, 2015.
David Linker	"How Pope Francis Is Perpetuating the Catholic Church's Radical Anti-Abortion Position," *The Week*, September 4, 2015.
Michael J. Miller	"Death with Dignity: Questions, Concerns, Dangers," *Catholic World Report*, February 1, 2015.
Faustina Fynn Nyame	"Why I Agree with the Pope on Family Planning—Up to a Point," *Guardian*, January 21, 2015.
Dustin Siggins	"Tired of Obamacare? Check Out This New Catholic Health-Sharing Option," Life Site News, February 20, 2015.
John-Henry Westen	"Pope Francis Eases Forgiveness of Abortion for Jubilee Year of Mercy," Life Site News, September 1, 2015.

OPPOSING
VIEWPOINTS®
SERIES

CHAPTER 3

What Are Issues Facing the Catholic Priesthood?

Chapter Preface

In 2013 the total number of Catholic priests worldwide was about 413,418. This was a notable increase from 2012's figure of 412,236, but it was still markedly lower than the number of priests in the early 1970s, when the church boasted about 419,728 priests worldwide. In the mid-2010s, these statistics were simply another part of a continuously changing reality for the Catholic Church: its priesthood had been suffering from a severe and steadily worsening shortage of priests.

This decline was occurring overwhelmingly in Western regions of the world such as Europe, the United States, and Oceania. In the United States particularly, the Catholic priesthood had in fact been in grave trouble for some time. In 1950 one Catholic priest served about 652 parishioners in an area; sixty years later, one priest served 1,652 parishioners. These statistics showed that even as the population of American Catholics increased over time, the number of priests being ordained to minister to them decreased.

Between 1975 and 2014, the number of Catholic priests in the United States fell from nearly 59,000 to about 38,200. Although this number was still substantially higher than the country's roughly 17,400 Catholic churches, the work to be done at each parish—including presiding over baptisms, funerals, and weddings; performing charity work; and teaching religious classes—was gradually becoming more demanding than only one priest could manage. Bishops who oversaw all the priests in a particular diocese reported that while retired or part-time priests assisted in performing parish work where they could, in general the American Catholic priest population was aging and dying faster than new priests were being ordained. Such was the case in many other Western countries as well.

As the shortage crisis continued in the mid-2010s, various members of the Catholic Church offered their own views of why fewer men were seeking the priesthood. Many blamed the problem on the church's sexual abuse scandals, which they claimed had disillusioned followers. Others posited that the church should permit married men as well as women to become priests, thereby bolstering the priesthood's dwindling ranks.

In 2015 American cardinal Raymond Leo Burke claimed the worldwide priest shortage was a response to the church allowing women to serve in more ministerial roles than in the past. For instance, permitting altar girls as well as altar boys to assist priests during liturgy, Burke said, afforded young men less opportunity to acquire firsthand experience of what Catholic priests do.

The following chapter presents opposing viewpoints on a number of issues related to the modern Catholic priesthood. Subjects covered include the issue of priestly celibacy, the ordination of female priests, and the church's response to sexual abuse scandals involving priests.

> *"Celibacy configures priests more completely to Christ, who lived a perfectly chaste life."*

Catholic Priests Should Remain Celibate

Stephen Beale

In the following viewpoint, Stephen Beale provides numerous reasons for why he believes celibacy for Catholic priests is important. He argues, for instance, that priests ought to be like Jesus, who himself was chaste. Beale also claims that celibacy should be viewed as a personal sacrifice made by priests, who should grow closer to God through doing so. Beale is a writer based in Providence, Rhode Island.

As you read, consider the following questions:

1. What term does Beale use to describe priests who try to be like Christ?

2. What does Beale say Christ did that priests should also do to attain purity?

3. What kind of Old Testament priests does Beale say modern Catholic priests should imitate?

To our sex-obsessed culture, priestly celibacy seems a hard teaching of the church, a heavy burden that must be borne with ascetic grit and iron resolve.

But that's not how the popes of the twentieth century saw it. In their words, celibacy is the "choicest ornament of our priesthood" (Pope Pius X), "one of the purest glories of the Catholic priesthood" (Pope Pius XI), and a discipline that makes the whole life of the priest "resound with the splendor of holy chastity" (Pope John XXIII). Such lofty words were inspired by the rich and profound theological reasons for a celibate priesthood—reasons worth bearing in mind as the old debate over it has flared up into the news. Here are ten of them.

1. Priests as Christ figures. Above all else, the Catholic priest is an *alter Christus*—"another Christ." This is clearest in the sacrifice of the Mass, when the priest acts in the person of the Christ in offering the Eucharist. Celibacy configures priests more completely to Christ, who lived a perfectly chaste life. Thus, they not only "participate in His priestly office" but also share "His very condition of living," Pope Paul VI writes in the encyclical *Sacerdotalis Caelibatus*.

2. Marriage to the church. In scripture, the church is often depicted as the bridegroom of Christ. In celibacy, the priest, as an *alter Christus*, witnesses through his life to the marriage of Christ to His church. "In virginity or celibacy, the human being is awaiting, also in a bodily way, the . . . marriage of Christ with the church, giving himself or herself completely to the church in the hope that Christ may give Himself to the church in the full truth of eternal life. The celibate person thus anticipates in his or her flesh the new world of the future resurrection," John Paul II writes in his apostolic constitution *Familiaris Consortio*.

3. Spiritual fatherhood. Through celibacy, priests give themselves over wholly to the service God and His church. Just as a father is uniquely dedicated to his children, so also the priest should be dedicated to his parishioners. As one Jesuit priest at Georgetown University recently put it in the *Washington Post*: "I do not have my own biological children, but I have over 6,000 here on Georgetown's main campus! I have many sons and daughters who call me 'Father.'" John Paul II describes this as a "singular sharing in God's fatherhood."

4. *Celibacy as sacrifice.* In renouncing married life, the priest also links himself with Christ's own sacrifice on the Cross. "In a similar way, by a daily dying to himself and by giving up the legitimate love of a family of his own for the love of Christ and of His kingdom, the priest will find the glory of an exceedingly rich and fruitful life in Christ, because like Him and in Him, he loves and dedicates himself to all the children of God," Paul VI writes. This ultimately is the purpose of human sexuality—to be "a genuine sign of and precious service to the love of communion and gift of self to others," writes Blessed Pope John Paul II in *Pastores Dabo Vobis*.

5. *Celibacy as angelic purity.* Celibacy is not only a sacrificial act. It is also a mark of purity. Just as Christ offered Himself as a pure and spotless victim, so should the priest. Moreover "a purity of heart and a sanctity of life" befit the "solemnity and holiness" of the office, Pope Pius XI writes in the encyclical *Ad Catholici Sacerdotii*. Some have described this otherworldly purity as angelic: "The priest must be so pure that, if he were to be lifted up and placed in the heavens themselves, he might take a place in the midst of the angels," St. John Chrysostom said.

6. *Loneliness as a link to Christ.* Even the loneliness a priest may experience may unite him more closely with Christ, according to Paul VI: "At times loneliness will weigh heavily on the priest, but he will not for that reason regret having generously chosen it. Christ, too, in the most tragic hours of His life was alone—abandoned by the very ones whom He had

Celibacy Allows Priests' First Priority to Be the Church

The image used to describe the role of the priest is one of marriage to the church. Just as marriage is the total gift of self to another, the priesthood requires the total gift of self to the church. A priest's first duty is to his flock, while a husband's first duty is to his wife. Obviously, these two roles will often conflict, as St. Paul noted and as many married priests will tell you. A celibate priest is able to give his undivided attention to his parishioners without the added responsibility of caring for his own family. They are able to pick up and go whenever necessary, whether this involves moving to a new parish or responding to a late-night crisis. Celibate priests are better able to respond to these frequent changes and demands on their time and attention.

"5 Arguments Against Priestly Celibacy and How to Refute Them," Catholic Education Resource Center.

chosen as witnesses to, and companions of, His life, and whom He had loved 'to the end'—but He stated, 'I am not alone, for the Father is with me.'"

7. Time for prayer. As much time as those in married time spend in prayer, priests should devote even more, church Fathers taught, according to Ukrainian Catholic theologian Roman Cholij. One basis for this view is 1 Corinthians 7:5, where St. Paul is giving advice to those who are married: "Do not deprive each other, except perhaps by mutual consent for a time, to be free for prayer, but then return to one another, so that Satan may not tempt you through your lack of self-control." It follows that priests, who do not have another person to "return" to, should have more time for prayer.

8. Perfection of the Israelite priesthood. Catholics look back to the Old Testament priests as forerunners. They understand that the priesthood did not end with Christ—it was reborn and renewed through Him. In the Old Testament, Levite priests were allowed to marry, but celibacy was required while they were serving in the sanctuary. For the church fathers, the Catholic priesthood was the "perfection" of the Levitical priesthood, according to Cholij. "Hence . . . if the Levites practised temporary continence when in the sanctuary, so much more should Christian priests, always ready to serve, practise continence," Cholij writes.

9. Detachment from the world. Celibacy is but one example of a broader detachment from all things of this world—something necessary in order for the priest "to follow the Divine Master more easily and readily," according to Pope Pius XII in his apostolic exhortation *Menti Nostrae.* "Sanctity alone makes us what our divine vocation demands, men crucified to the world and to whom the world has been crucified, men walking in newness of life who . . . seek only heavenly things and strive by every means to lead others to them," Pius X writes in his apostolic exhortation, *Haerent Animo.*

10. A living sign of heaven. In heaven, men will neither marry nor will women be given in marriage—instead, they will be like the angels, as Christ says in Matthew 22:30. In a special way, celibacy makes priests living witnesses to this future reality. As Paul VI put it, priestly celibacy "proclaims the presence on earth of the final stages of salvation with the arrival of a new world, and in a way it anticipates the fulfillment of the kingdom as it sets forth its supreme values which will one day shine forth in all the children of God."

| *"A married priest can be just as holy and dedicated as a single priest."*

Catholic Priests Should Be Allowed to Marry

Dan Delzell

In the following viewpoint, Dan Delzell argues that marriage is a healthy goal for anyone to pursue and that the Catholic Church should not deny its priests the opportunity to marry. Doing so, he claims, could cause the priests undue suffering in their lives, as they are forced to long continuously for a happiness that can never be attained. Marriage, Delzell believes, could help priests grow substantially in spirituality and help them to be better Christians. Delzell is the pastor of Wellspring Lutheran Church in Papillion, Nebraska.

As you read, consider the following questions:

1. What offense does Delzell believe the Catholic Church is committing against young, aspiring priests in forcing them to remain celibate?

2. From what source does Delzell say most Christians believe the requirement of priestly celibacy descends?

3. What principle found in the Gospel does Delzell believe Christians should always try to preserve?

C hristians are people who trust in Christ's death for their salvation rather than their own religious deeds. They not only trust in Jesus as their Savior, but they also follow Him as their Lord. The Gospel message is the foundation of the Christian faith. And it produces a life of freedom in Christ.

With that being said, the choice to marry or remain single should be enjoyed by all believers, including Catholic priests. What if, for example, a priest changes his mind about celibacy based on scripture or for personal reasons? It goes against the spirit of the Gospel to forbid him from pursuing this wholesome desire for marriage, whether he comes to this decision early on or later in life. It simply contradicts Christian freedom to bind man's conscience in this way, especially with something as beautiful as marriage.

Priestly Celibacy Is Cruel

There is certainly nothing wrong with remaining celibate. If you are happy to do so in your service for the Lord, then great. But to require Christians, and even ministers at that, to remain celibate is not in line with grace or truth. In fact, the apostle Paul addressed how dangerous it is to "forbid people to marry" (1 Timothy 4:3). God's Word also declares that "it is better to marry than to burn with passion" (1 Cor. 7:9). The New Testament even instructs ministers to "be the husband of one wife" (1 Timothy 3:2).

So what's really going on with this "lifetime ban from marriage" so to speak? By convincing aspiring priests to agree to a life of celibacy, it could be argued that a form of spiritual abuse is actually taking place against impressionable young men. In their zeal, these devout apprentices agree to submit to this troublesome regulation because they want to be "good Catholics." And what better way to be a good Catholic than to be a priest, right? Or so goes the thinking. But look at all the good Catholics who are married. Why shouldn't their priests be afforded the same opportunity? Wouldn't that be in everyone's best interest?

Try to take a step back for a second and look at the Christian church as a whole around the world. Then ask yourself: Does the Holy Spirit truly desire only celibate ministers for just one branch of Christ's church, while desiring both single and married ministers for most of the other branches? Seriously. Do you realize how crazy and out of sync that sounds?

If it is such a wise and godly idea, why aren't a significant number of Christian churches being led by the Holy Spirit to require their pastors to be celibate? The answer is obvious. The vast majority of Christians throughout the world do not believe this requirement comes from the Holy Spirit, but rather merely from tradition. Interestingly, the Catholic Church recognizes as well that celibacy is only a tradition.

Why Priestly Marriage Is Good

With those considerations in mind, there are a boatload of good reasons why young Catholic men should not be required to sign away their right to get married later in life. Here are just 10 of the many reasons.

1. God instituted marriage and it is therefore very good.

2. Marriage teaches ministers a lot about the Christian life.

3. Parenting is an important aspect in the life of discipleship.

4. Binding man's conscience on secondary matters is harmful.

5. A married priest can be just as holy and dedicated as a single priest.

6. God leads many ministers of the Gospel around the world to get married.

Priestly Celibacy in Question

Pope Francis hinted this past weekend [in July 2014] that he is working on a "solution" to priestly celibacy, a move that could signal a possible shift in opinions—if not religious law—around the Catholic church's practice of barring clergy from marrying. . . .

But the question remains: does the pope really want to change the church's policy on priestly celibacy, and if he does, is that even within his power?

At least one of those questions is easy to answer: yes, Francis can change the church's policy. Priestly celibacy is only canon law, or a man-made rule, and not church dogma or doctrine. Priestly celibacy didn't even exist in early Christianity, with several early popes . . . , bishops, and priests marrying and fathering children during the church's first three centuries. The tradition of clerical continence doesn't show up until the Council of Elvira around 305–306 CE. . . .

Many defenders of celibacy point to the fact that Jesus didn't have a wife, and since priests are meant to emulate the example of Christ, marriage is thought to be suspect. But Jesus also spoke Aramaic, was Middle Eastern, and wore primitive clothing—things hard to find among many of today's Catholic priests—and one of his disciples, Peter, is listed as having a mother-in-law. And while the Apostle Paul writes in 1 Corinthians 7:7–8 that "I wish that all were as I myself am," meaning celibate, even he refrains from making it a hard-and-fast rule. He goes on to add the following caveat a few verses later. "But if they are not practicing self-control, then they should marry. For it is better to marry than to be aflame with passion."

Jack Jenkins, "Is Pope Francis Going to Let Priests Get Married?," ThinkProgress, July 14, 2014.

7. Doing something "for the sake of tradition" is not always a good enough reason.

8. Priests would personally learn a lot about the equality between husband and wife.

9. Many wise and discerning Christians in the Catholic Church believe priests should marry.

10. The Gospel message of forgiveness through Christ is more important than marriage or celibacy.

"Where the Spirit of the Lord is there is freedom" (2 Cor. 3:17). Don't you just love the freedom which is found in the Gospel. There is nothing like it, and we must do our best to preserve it as we go about our lives of Christian discipleship.

Hope for the Future

Maybe the new pope will breathe a breath of fresh air on the matter into the Catholic system. The pope's example often seems to set the tone in their church. It will be interesting to see how he chooses to address this particular regulation in his organization.

The pope could really shake things up by getting married himself. After all, there is nothing in the Bible which forbids him from doing so. I read yesterday [September 21, 2013] that the pope was given a used car by a priest in northern Italy which he intends to drive around for short commutes on Vatican grounds. Hey, marriage isn't much tougher than driving. Well, maybe just a little bit. But it sure satisfies man's desire for a soul mate.

When considering marriage and celibacy, as with other matters of the Christian life, we would be wise to always remember, "It is for freedom that Christ has set us free" (Galatians 5:1).

> "As bread and wine are the matter for the sacrament of the Eucharist, a man is the matter for the sacrament of ordination."

Women Should Never Be Ordained Catholic Priests

Dwight Longenecker

In the following viewpoint, Dwight Longenecker argues that the Catholic Church should never ordain women as priests. The reason for this, he claims, is that the church simply does not possess the spiritual authority to alter what God himself, through Jesus, instituted on Earth. Just as Jesus chose all male disciples to build his early church, Longenecker believes, so, too, must the modern Catholic Church ordain only men to represent God to the rest of the world. Longenecker is a parish priest at Our Lady of the Rosary Church in Greenville, South Carolina.

As you read, consider the following questions:

1. What does Longenecker say were some past attempts to prove that female priests served in the early Catholic Church?

2. What does Longenecker say was C.S. Lewis's belief about changing God's priestly representation at the liturgy?

3. What does Longenecker propose as an alternative to expecting Catholic doctrine on the priesthood to change?

Eleven years ago [2002] Christine Mayr Lumetzberger was excommunicated because she attempted to be ordained as a Catholic priest. A mischievous and misleading article by British journalist Peter Stanford entitled "Meet the Female Priest Defying Catholicism for Her Faith" recounts her story.

Ms. Lumetzberger says she knew from childhood she was called to be a priest. She joined a convent, but after leaving to marry a divorced man, she decided to become a priest. In 2002 she joined six other women on a boat on the Danube and was "ordained." A few years later she claims to have been consecrated as a bishop. She refuses to name the bishops who consecrated her, no mention is made of her formation or training to be a priest, much less a bishop, but Stanford makes it clear that Lumetzberger is a brave pioneer—a woman of faith who has defied the "celibate men who ... give no explanation of why these laws should be followed except fear."

Stanford's sentimental and shallow tribute to Lumetzberger gives the usual self-righteous arguments for women priests combined with zero theological rationale or evidence of any knowledge of the church's real reasons for rejecting female ordination. Instead we are given a soft image of a "serene" and "softly spoken" woman who helps the poor and has a smiling "mumsy" image.

Despite the clear teachings of Popes Paul VI, John Paul II, Benedict XVI and Francis ruling out the ordination of women, Catholics of a certain strain still press for the innovation and insist that more discussion is needed, more dialogue is required and yet more listening is necessary.

Is, in fact, more discussion necessary—or is the matter settled?

The Anglican Story

To understand the women's ordination debate in the Catholic Church it is instructive to see the issue in the wider ecumenical context. The push for women's ordination began in the Anglican Communion. Although a Chinese woman, Florence Li Tim-Oi, had been ordained in Hong Kong in 1944 because of a post-war lack of priests, the first women priests were not formally recognized in Hong Kong until 1971. Three years later, in the United States, eleven women were ordained illegally and were followed the next year by four more. Then in 1976 the Episcopal Church approved the ordination of women, to be followed eventually by most of the Anglican national churches around the world. The Church of England finally joined the other Anglicans and ordained their first women priests in 1994—just fifty years after the emergency ordination of Florence Li Tim-Oi.

The ordination of women in the 1970s was not a sudden and unforeseen event. The Anglicans had been debating the issue since the 1940s. C.S. Lewis contributed a prescient essay on the subject in 1948 entitled "Priestesses in the Church," which states most of the strongest arguments against women's ordination. Lewis points out that the arguments in favor are at first glance utilitarian and sensible. In other words, "We have a shortage of priests. Women can do the job as well as men, why should they be denied the opportunity?"

Over the years, the utilitarian argument was supplemented by the sentimental argument and the argument from justice. The sentimental argument played up the niceness of the women who claimed to be called to the priesthood and portrayed them as victims of the oppressive patriarchal establishment, while the argument from justice was based on egalitarian principles latent within the women's liberation movement.

Those in favor of the innovation could not use specific texts from scripture to support their case. Indeed all the relevant texts, such as 1 Timothy 2:12—"I do not allow a woman to teach or hold authority over a man in church"—dictated against women's ordination. Instead they argued from St. Paul's larger principles, "In Christ there is neither male nor female" (Galatians 3:28), and used the story of Peter's vision in Acts 10 to justify innovations which at first seemed illicit, but which were spirit led. There were also attempts to prove that there were female priests in the early church. A wall painting from the catacombs seemed to show a woman praying in the *orans* position with arms extended in a priestly fashion. Other scholars tried to prove there was a female apostle in the New Testament named Junia (see Romans 16:7).

The Catholic Story

While the Anglicans debated women's ordination, the Catholic authorities also looked into the matter. Catholic teaching on the question shadowed the developments in the Anglican Church step by step. So it was in 1976—the same year that the Episcopal Church in the U.S. voted to ordain women—that the Sacred Congregation for the Doctrine of the Faith issued the Declaration on the Question of the Admission of Women to the Ministerial Priesthood. The key teaching from the congregation was that the church does not have the authority to ordain women as priests due to the church's determination to remain faithful to her constant tradition, her fidelity to Christ's will, and the iconic value of male representation which is linked to the "sacramental nature" of the priesthood.

C.S. Lewis's essay, written some twenty years beforehand, unpacks what this means. Lewis explained that a priest speaks to God for the people and speaks to the people for God. No one would have a problem with a woman doing the former, but there is a problem with a woman doing the latter. In other words, if the priest represents God in the drama of the liturgy, and a woman takes that place, an important element of the iconography of worship is altered. As a literary expert, Lewis explains that changing our representation of God in worship alters our understanding of God. When you change a word or image, you must also change the meaning.

As usual, Lewis puts it very plainly, "Suppose the reformer stops saying that a good woman may be like God and begins saying that God is like a good woman. Suppose he says that we might just as well pray to 'Our Mother which art in heaven' as to 'Our Father'. Suppose he suggests that the incarnation might just as well have taken a female as a male form, and the second person of the Trinity be as well called the daughter as the son. Suppose, finally, that the mystical marriage were reversed, that the church were the bridegroom and Christ the bride. All this, as it seems to me, is involved in the claim that a woman can represent God as a priest does."

No Church Authority

The term "the sacramental nature of the priesthood" seems to be misunderstood by a good number of Catholics. The proponents of women's ordination characterize the church's position as, "the church says women can't be priests because Jesus only chose men to be priests. That was then. This is now. Things change." This is to trivialize the argument. The reasoning cuts deeper to the basic understanding of the sacraments and the relationship between Christ and his church. Put simply, the church does not have the authority, even for seemingly good historical and cultural reasons, to change the sacraments which Christ himself instituted.

So, for example, if a missionary goes to a primitive tribe that knows nothing of wine and bread, but has fermented coconut juice and manioc root bread as staples, the priest cannot celebrate Mass using coconut juice and manioc root bread. The sacrament is invalid if the matter is incorrect. The church

Only Men Can Be Priests

The *Catechism of the Catholic Church* states that only men can receive holy orders because Jesus chose men as his apostles and the "apostles did the same when they chose collaborators to succeed them in their ministry." John Paul II wrote in 1994 that this teaching is definitive and not open to debate among Catholics.

Yet some Catholics persist in asking why, as traditional distinctions between the sexes break down in many areas of society, the Catholic clergy must remain an exclusively male vocation, and what this suggests about the church's understanding of women's worth and dignity.

Francis X. Rocca,
"Why Not Women Priests? The Papal Theologian Explains,"
Catholic News Service, January 31, 2013.

does not have the authority to alter the matter of the sacrament—even for what seem to be good reasons. As bread and wine are the matter for the sacrament of the Eucharist, a man is the matter for the sacrament of ordination. As four popes have made clear, the church does not have the authority to change the matter of the sacrament of ordination. She cannot undo what the Lord has done.

Therefore in 1994, the same year the Church of England voted to ordain women, Pope John Paul II re-affirmed the 1976 teaching. In his letter *Ordinatio Sacerdotalis* he wrote, "Wherefore, in order that all doubt may be removed regarding a matter of great importance. . . . I declare that the church has no authority whatsoever to confer priestly ordination on women and that this judgment is to be definitively held by all the church's faithful." After repeated questioning, Cardinal Joseph Ratzinger, then head of the Sacred Congregation for the

Doctrine of the Faith, affirmed twice in writing that Pope John Paul II's teaching was definitive. Nevertheless, somewhat befuddled by the statement, Archbishop of Canterbury George Carey replied, "We would like to seek further clarification."

The Never Ending Story

Carey's confused request for further clarification seems to be echoed among the Catholics who continue to press for women's ordination. When asked about this issue in a press conference, Pope Francis affirmed the teaching of his predecessors with another very clear statement. "The door to women's ordination is closed."

Why then do women like Christine Mayr Lumetzberger continue to present themselves as Catholic women priests? Why do journalists like Peter Stanford continue to pretend that this is a relevant and vital issue in the Catholic Church? Why do Catholic scholars continue to argue for women's ordination while dissident priests and religious sisters support groups like Women's Ordination Worldwide, Catholic Women's Ordination and Roman Catholic Womenpriests?

Since 2002, Roman Catholic Womenpriests has "ordained" women as deacons, priests and bishops, claiming that these ordinations are valid because the first ordinations were done by a validly ordained Catholic male bishop (Romulo Antonio Braschi, who left the Roman Catholic Church in 1975). What kind of Catholics are these who persist, knowing that their ordinations are invalid and that they are excommunicated by their actions? What do they believe they will accomplish?

The Catholics who are operating in this way are working within a hermeneutic of revolution. Guided by the principles of protest and dissent, they believe that the Catholic Church must change. Guided by ideology rather than theology and by a Hegelian [referring to followers of Georg Wilhelm Friedrich Hegel] philosophy of conflict rather than the Magisterium [teaching authority especially of the Catholic Church], they see the issue of women's ordination as a great struggle for justice through which they will eventually prevail. The clear statements from the church on this matter only serve to give them something to dispute and dismiss.

What is most tiresome about this never ending story is that anyone who reads ecclesiastical history will soon realize that change in the Catholic Church never occurs through the Hegelian struggle. Male-only ordination has been defined as a doctrine of the church and it cannot be changed. What can happen, however, is for doctrine to develop. Our understanding of priesthood can grow away from the entrenched clericalism into which we too often fall, and at the same time our understanding of women's ministry in the church can continue to develop.

On the question of women's ordination however, Catholics should be clear: *Roma Locuta Est—Causa Finita Est*. Rome has spoken. That settles it.

> *"The Catholic Church lags far behind the world's major religions when it comes to equality between men and women."*

Women Should Be Allowed to Become Catholic Priests

Jo Piazza

In the following viewpoint, Jo Piazza argues that the Catholic Church is outdated in not allowing women to be ordained priests. Women, she believes, possess just as much, or even more, potential than men to hold positions of leadership in the church. Piazza justifies her opinion by claiming that even Jesus himself regarded women as important figures in his ministry. Piazza is a journalist whose work has appeared in the Wall Street Journal, *the* New York Times, *and numerous other publications. She is the author of* If Nuns Ruled the World: Ten Sisters on a Mission.

As you read, consider the following questions:

1. What two other religious denominations does Piazza cite as examples of progression on the issue of women priests?

2. What fraction of Anglican clerics does Piazza say are women?

3. What does Piazza say the feminist Sister Donna Quinn does to show the world that women's voices are unfairly excluded from the papal conclave?

Sometimes I imagine a Catholic Church where pedophile priests were rightfully punished and defrocked rather than slapped on the hand and relocated; a Catholic Church where billions of dollars in investments and property were reallocated to help the poor; a Catholic Church where ego was replaced by open and honest communication.

It's even harder, sometimes, to imagine a Catholic Church that gives women the respect and leadership positions they deserve. Women's ordination in the Catholic Church was one of the few feminist movements to emerge from the '70s that hit a complete and total stalemate. It is the most radical and ignored issue in the institution right now.

In the months leading up to Christmas in 1974, a progressive Catholic feminist named Mary Lynch sent out, instead of seasonal greetings, a note asking her acquaintances if they thought it was time that the church allowed women to be priests. 31 of the women and one of the men responded yes.

The next year Lynch organized the first Women's Ordination Conference in Detroit to examine the issue. She expected a few hundred participants at best and got more than 2,000.

In the process of writing my book *If Nuns Ruled the World*, I met Sister Maureen Fiedler, now the host of the public radio program *Interfaith Voices*. In 1979 she helped to organize the "Stand Up for Women" demonstration at Pope John Paul II's first papal visit to the United States, in which 53 Catholic sisters wore blue armbands and refused to sit down while the pope spoke.

Wearing a brown suit and a jaunty checkered blouse, Sister Theresa Kane addressed the pope. "I urge you, Your Holiness, to respond to the voices coming from the women of this country who are desirous of serving in and with the church as fully participating members," Kane said.

35 years have passed and little has changed.

Ongoing Deadlock

Pope Francis, still shiny and new in the Vatican, has been hailed as a potential reformer, superstar and progressive icon since he was elected to the position by a conclave of men last year [in 2013]. And yet, on the subject of women he has held fast to the church's institutional antiquated stance—women can't be priests.

"The reservation of the priesthood to males, as a sign of Christ the spouse who gives himself in the Eucharist, is not a question open to discussion," he said in his first apostolic exhortation in November 2013. He added that he wanted women to use their "feminine genius" to contribute to the church in other ways.

God forbid that women use their feminine genius to actually lead in an institution that has been plagued by decades of public relations crises, mainly perpetuated by male leaders who have used their masculine genius in shameful ways.

Today, on Women's Equality Day, it's worth noting that the Catholic Church lags far behind the world's major religions when it comes to equality between men and women.

In 1972, the Jewish Reform movement ordained Sally J. Priesand as America's first female rabbi. In 1974, the "Philadelphia Eleven" caused a firestorm within the Episcopal Church when eleven female deacons presented themselves to three male bishops to be ordained as priests.

The Church of England has allowed women to become priests for 20 years, and around one-third of Anglican clerics are women. In June [2014], the Anglican Church voted to al-

The Call for Women Priests

After serving as a Roman Catholic priest for 40 years, I was expelled from the priesthood last November because of my public support for the ordination of women.

Catholic priests say that the call to be a priest comes from God. As a young priest, I began to ask myself and my fellow priests: "Who are we, as men, to say that our call from God is authentic, but God's call to women is not?" Isn't our all-powerful God, who created the cosmos, capable of empowering a woman to be a priest?

Let's face it. The problem is not with God, but with an all-male clerical culture that views women as lesser than men. Though I am not optimistic, I pray that the newly elected Pope Francis will rethink this antiquated and unholy doctrine. . . .

A *New York Times*/CBS poll this month [March 2013] reported that 70 percent of Catholics in the United States believed that Pope Francis should allow women to be priests. . . .

I have but one simple request for our new pope. I respectfully ask that he announce to the 1.2 billion Catholics around the world: "For many years we have been praying for God to send us more vocations to the priesthood. Our prayers have been answered. Our loving God, who created us equal, is calling women to be priests in our church. Let us welcome them and give thanks to God."

Roy Bourgeois, "My Prayer: Let Women Be Priests,"
New York Times, *March 20, 2013.*

low women to finally become bishops: this from a faith that broke from the Catholic Church so that a monarch might be allowed to divorce his wife.

The True Place of Women

The Bible tells us that Christ surrounded himself with strong and opinionated women. The first person that Jesus encountered when he rose from the dead was none other than Mary Magdalene. Only then did she tell the men about it.

"The problem is that those Gospels are written in a way that doesn't give women enough credit," Sister Maureen told me. "I actually think that in the early church—and by that I mean the first century or two—women were close to being equals of men. I think it is one of the suppressed realities in church history."

I asked Sister Donna Quinn, an ardent feminist activist and crusader for women's reproductive rights who has volunteered as an escort at an Illinois abortion clinic, what she thought about the new pope.

"How many women were on the ballot? How many women voted for this pope or ever vote for the leadership in the church?" Sister Donna asked. She's since started a campaign of burning pink smoke around the country to underscore the point that women had been left out of the conclave.

"I don't think most people understand the significance of the fact that women have no right to vote in the Catholic Church," she added. "The church has put us down and tried to keep us down, and it's one of the biggest institutions in the world."

Much has been made of Pope Francis's savvy about the contemporary world. He takes selfies. He's on Twitter. He must realize that the church does itself a great disservice in keeping women out of positions of power.

It's time, I think, that we reminded him that "feminine genius" won't cut it. If you're on Twitter, wish him a happy Women's Equality Day: you can find him @Pontifex.

> "The church must fully answer for its past failure to protect children from the clergy entrusted to shape their moral and spiritual development."

Catholic Church's Stance Against Clerical Abuse Not Enough

Lauren Carasik

In the following viewpoint, Lauren Carasik argues that the Catholic Church must take more aggressive steps both to answer for past sexual abuse by its priests and to prevent further abuse from occurring. She writes that in the past, the church has vacillated on correcting the issue, never implementing firm, comprehensive reforms that would root out the problem permanently. Carasik believes that the church should submit itself completely to outside corrective measures that would ensure no sexual abuse by priests goes unpunished. Carasik is a clinical professor of law at Western New England University School of Law in Springfield, Massachusetts.

As you read, consider the following questions:

1. For what four offenses does Carasik say abuse survivor groups have criticized the Vatican?

2. On what three other secular issues did the United Nations suggest the Catholic Church change its position?

3. What long-delayed action does Carasik recommend the church take to break its former code of silence on priestly abuse?

Urging a sprawling religious institution to take immediate remedial action to redress a scourge of pervasive sexual abuse within its ranks is unlikely to generate global controversy. Unless that organization is the Catholic Church and the edict is issued by a secular watchdog and muddied by the Vatican's unique status as a hybrid sovereign state ruled by its own religious laws and mores.

A Suffering Public Image

On Feb. 5, the United Nations [U.N.] Committee on the Rights of the Child issued a stern rebuke of the Holy See for its failure to comply with its international obligations under the Convention on the Rights of the Child. The panel's observations in its second periodic report on the Vatican accused it of systematically protecting pedophile priests and showing greater concern for preserving its own reputation and protecting the perpetrators than for upholding the best interests of the children. It called on the church to remove abusive clergy from official duty, turn abusers and those who shielded them over to state authorities for prosecution and release its voluminous archives of sexual abuse complaints.

The U.N. report has reignited a lingering debate between defenders of the church and critics who deplore its handling of the sex abuse crisis. Survivor groups and their supporters hailed the report as a watershed development in their arduous and lengthy battle to seek redress for past and ongoing abuses as well as efforts to prevent future ones. They have long criticized the Vatican for hiding behind a stony and impenetrable wall of secrecy, obstructing justice, protecting abusers and punishing whistle-blowers.

Barbara Dorris, outreach director for Survivors Network of Those Abused by Priests [SNAP], lauded the report's long overdue attention to a troubling issue for which the church has never publicly answered.

The church has also been censured for its utter failure to acknowledge the incalculable toll of these crimes, including the staggering number of victims, the global reach and the lasting and profound nature of the harm inflicted on victims.

"Limited Legal Authority"

The report drew an initially curt official response from the Vatican spokesman, who said the Holy See would study the document closely, according to the precepts of international law. Subsequent comments by officials and their surrogates doubled down, casting doubt on the report's accuracy and legitimacy.

The Vatican's U.N. ambassador Archbishop Silvano Tomasi decried the committee's failure to take into account the reforms that the Holy See has already implemented, suggesting that the report may have been written before church officials appeared before the committee last month and clarified its actions. The Vatican claims that cases of abuse have been sharply reduced. But it declined to answer the committee's request for data on abuse investigations and statistics, stating that the church released such information only when required by legal proceedings.

Critics note that the Vatican's claim of comprehensive reforms was undermined by lapses in its policies and procedures that belie its public proclamations. In 2010 the church conceded that its hierarchy does not require bishops to report abuse to authorities. Instead, it defers to local laws to dictate reporting policy, thereby abdicating its responsibility to assist in identifying, removing and punishing predatory priests.

In a recent instance of elevating self-interest over the needs of victims, last year the Catholic Church in California lobbied against proposed changes to California's civil statute of limitations. The bill would have granted sexual abuse victims who missed an earlier deadline a one-year extension to file lawsuits because of the delayed discovery of psychological problems resulting from abuse. Evidence demonstrates that survivors often need years to come to grips with the trauma and develop the resilience and determination necessary to endure the pain and stigma of seeking redress.

The Holy See claimed it possesses limited legal authority to dictate the conduct of its clergy outside the geographical boundaries of tiny Vatican City. Critics call this defense disingenuous, and the U.N. committee agreed, concluding that the Vatican is the "supreme power of the Catholic Church," in which "subordinates in Catholic religious orders are bound by obedience to the Pope."

Internal Intrusion?

Supporters of the church say the report was distorted by special interest groups and that the committee's ideological bias blurred the distinction between universally held norms and ideological preferences. In addition to addressing sexual abuse, the report urged the church to consider how the rights of children are affected by its teachings on sexual orientation, given the violence perpetrated against adolescent members of the lesbian, gay, bisexual and transgender community and discrimination against children of same-sex parents. It also raised the issues of reproductive health, abortion and gender equality. The Vatican and supporters pointedly rejected the U.N.'s suggestions for changes to core church doctrine, which they deem sacrosanct and protected by religious freedom.

Some observers predict that the committee's inclusion of these contested topics will blunt the impact of the report. While commending the U.N.'s attention to the issue of child sexual abuse, Sister Mary Ann Walsh of the U.S. [Conference of Catholic Bishops] said the committee lost credibility by venturing into the culture wars.

But credibility cuts both ways, and the church's selective willingness to mete out discipline against its bishops sheds an unflattering light on its internal priorities. As NPR's senior European correspondent Sylvia Poggioli quipped, "Speaking out publicly in favor of women's ordination, for example, has triggered removal (of a bishop). Not so for covering up sex abuse of minors."

Last month, Bishop Charles J. Scicluna, the Vatican's former chief prosecutor on sex crimes, told the U.N. committee, "It is not a policy of the Holy See to encourage cover-ups. This is against the truth." Yet the Vatican's efforts to cast the scandal as history and claiming that the church now gets it was undercut by contradictory signals from the church. As Scicluna was testifying in Geneva, Pope Francis was celebrating Mass and meeting privately in Rome with Cardinal Roger

M. Mahony, the disgraced former archbishop of Los Angeles who was publicly accused of protecting abusive priests.

Full Accountability

The church claims it is taking unparalleled efforts to protect children. But the sex abuse scandal became public only through persistent and courageous efforts of survivors and their advocates who came forward to demand justice and protect others. Hence the church's mea culpa [admission of fault] was forced, at a considerable cost to those who suffered sexual violence at the hands of church officials and were often re-victimized in telling the truth of their experiences.

It is not enough to prevent future abuse: The church must fully answer for its past failure to protect children from the clergy entrusted to shape their moral and spiritual development. The Vatican must fully cooperate with prosecutors in seeking accountability for abusers and for those whose misguided protection enabled priests to continue inflicting unspeakable damage on young victims. The church must open its archives to shatter the code of silence that shrouded this shameful scandal in secrecy and continues to impede truth and justice.

It would be a shame if the report's inclusion of sexual orientation, gender equality and reproductive health is used to undermine the legitimacy of its withering critique of the systematic protection of pedophiles. The countless young and vulnerable victims of this church deserve better.

*"Under Francis's leadership, the Vatican
has taken some steps toward reform,
including criminalizing sexual abuse
and forming an advisory board."*

The Catholic Church Is
Progressing Toward Clerical
Abuse Reform

Priyanka Boghani

*In the following viewpoint, Jason Berry, in an interview with
Priyanka Boghani, argues that Pope Francis has taken more
steps to hold the Catholic Church responsible for priestly sexual
abuse than several of his predecessors. He has done this, Berry
claims, by hearing the stories of the abused and implementing
new church laws that will hold abusive priests accountable for
their actions. Berry believes that although Pope Francis is only
just beginning to work on this issue, he is moving in the right
direction. Priyanka Boghani is an author for PBS's* Frontline
*documentary television series. Jason Berry is an author and a re-
ligion writer at GlobalPost.*

As you read, consider the following questions:

1. How does Berry say Pope Francis used language to communicate with sexual abuse victims?

2. What kind of corrective legal system does Berry say the Catholic Church needs instead of canon law?

3. With what two democratic institutions does Berry claim the bishops who covered up the church's sexual abuse cases collided?

Yesterday [July 7, 2014], Pope Francis met for the first time in his papacy with victims who suffered childhood sexual abuse at the hands of clergy members. In a sermon at a private Mass for the victims, the pope used "some of his most emotional language yet," speaking "like a sinner in confession," wrote Jason Berry, religion writer at GlobalPost and author of *Render unto Rome: The Secret Life of Money in the Catholic Church*.

Frontline spoke with Berry this afternoon to find out more about Francis's meeting with the victims, what his record in Argentina suggests about his current intentions, and the prospects for his efforts to reform the Vatican.

Berry coproduced *Secrets of the Vatican, Frontline*'s inside look at the recent scandals that have rocked the church. . . .

A New Direction?

[Priyanka Boghani:] What was different about what Pope Francis did yesterday?

[Jason Berry] First, Pope Francis spent a great deal of time, according to the press reports, with each of the individuals. The young woman who spoke to the Irish newspapers said he was unhurried, he didn't look at his watch, and sat with her at length and listened to her. This was different from the approach that Pope Benedict took, with shorter meetings, and not as involved in gathering the emotional weight of each one of their accounts. I don't mean that as a criticism of the former pope, but Francis decided to go more than the extra mile in spending time with them.

The second point is, his language struck me as quite a reflection of guilt on his part on behalf of the hierarchy of the church. He begged for forgiveness rather like a sinner going to confession. What's significant there is that when someone in his position establishes a terrain of language, a territorial vocabulary, for discussing something that's as aching and reaching as this scandal that has been building for years, it creates a kind of arena for ongoing exchanges.

Even though some of the survivors' groups are attacking him, he's actually done them a favor by speaking as bluntly as he did. The challenge for the pope and for the Vatican now is how they create the structural changes to meet the promise of the rhetoric.

What does Pope Francis's record as Cardinal Jorge Mario Bergoglio in Argentina suggest about his current intentions?

His record in Argentina on this issue was certainly not good. I've read several media accounts, and there's no record that prior to yesterday he had ever met with an abuse victim. He supported a special report that was written in defense of the priest who had been convicted—Julio César Grassi. At least from what we know, Francis was not as egregious as say Cardinal [Bernard] Law in Boston or [Cardinal Roger] Mahony [former archbishop of Los Angeles].

Francis was certainly not a reformer on this issue before he became pope, and he did not position himself as a listener, a healer or someone on the side of the abused. What intrigues me about him as a man is that he's a work in progress—he shows a great capacity to change. I think Francis is on a journey, and he's using language to stake out territory for reform. The real question is, how much of a change agent will he prove to be?

Moves Toward Reform?

Under Francis's leadership, the Vatican has taken some steps toward reform, including criminalizing sexual abuse and forming an advisory board. Most recently, the Vatican defrocked former ambassador to the Dominican Republic, Archbishop Józef Wesolowski. Do these steps show a real intent to tackle the crisis, or are they mostly gestures to placate victims?

I don't think they're gestures. I think they do signal an intent on his part to go beyond what his predecessors did, or failed to do, and try to implement genuine reforms.

The issue he's facing can be boiled down to this: The Vatican does not have an adequate system of justice. Canon law works fine as an administrative mechanism, but when it comes to criminal procedures, when it comes to a bona fide rule of law as we have in democratic countries—the Vatican needs that kind of independent judiciary, leadership and hierarchy.

Francis has moved in that direction with the law he promulgated last year, under which the former envoy to the Dominican Republic has been held accountable. [Wesolowski] has two months to appeal, and the real question is what happens if the guilt is upheld: Will they remand him for a trial in Italy? Will they impose criminal penalties where he's actually put in a prison in Vatican City or in Rome? This is territory we have not seen before, but I think they're steps in the right direction.

The Road Ahead

If Francis were to push ahead with reforms, from what quarters would he face the most serious opposition?

Cardinals and bishops. Holding aside any judgment on my part of how badly a number of those men have performed, their attitude probably goes something like this: They didn't have leadership from John Paul II on this. He avoided the crisis. He was in enormous denial about it, and he didn't deal with it.

The lawsuits, the scandals, the prosecutions kept building, mainly in the English-speaking countries in the 1980s and 1990s. Finally, between Ireland and the United States there were so many of these earthquakes that when the *Boston Globe* series began in 2002, John Paul—ill though he was from Parkinson's—realized that he had to do something. The American cardinals went to Rome in the spring of 2002. Nothing really happened after that. There was no reform mechanism, there was no sweeping change—except they did start to defrock some of the worst perpetrators.

A lot of these bishops were acting under a business-as-usual mentality that had been in existence for decades, centuries. No one assumed that the church's internal business would ever come under the harsh spotlight or microscope of a prosecutor or civil court. That monarchical mentality of the bishops collided with two democratic institutions: the court system and the free press. Many probably thought we were doing what we were expected to. This pope comes along and starts punishing these bishops, instituting procedures to remove these men, and this seems to be what he is saying.

That is certainly what [advocates in Mexico, in Argentina, at SNAP (Survivors Network of Those Abused by Priests)] want; they want a judicial mechanism to remove bishops who've been grossly complicit. So, Francis is walking a tight rope.

Periodical and Internet Sources Bibliography

The following articles have been selected to supplement the diverse views presented in this chapter.

John L. Allen Jr.	"Why Pope Francis Won't Let Women Become Priests," *Time*, March 6, 2015.
Tracy Connor	"Wife, Grandma, Catholic Priest? Rebel Women Defy Church Ban," NBC News, January 19, 2015.
Rachel Donadio	"On Gay Priests, Pope Asks, 'Who Am I to Judge?,'" *New York Times*, July 30, 2013.
Andrea Gagliarducci	"Pope Francis Completes New Vatican Office to Tackle Clergy Abuse," Catholic News Agency, January 23, 2015.
Melinda Henneberger	"Pope Francis Should Consider Ending Celibacy as a Way of Healing Divisions," *Washington Post*, May 27, 2014.
The Hill	"Pope: Church's Credibility Rests on Its Responses to Clerical Sex Abuse," April 8, 2013.
Dwight Longenecker	"Catholic 'Women Priests': Can There Be a Discussion?," *Catholic World Report*, December 10, 2014.
Dwight Longenecker	"The Pope, Women Priests and Pedophiles," Patheos, January 24, 2015.
Michael Paulson	"Group of Catholic and Orthodox Officials Endorses Marriage for Some Priests," *New York Times*, June 6, 2014.
Reuters	"Meet the Catholic Priest Who Doesn't Believe in Celibacy," January 15, 2015.

OPPOSING
VIEWPOINTS®
SERIES

CHAPTER 4

How Should the Catholic Church Interact with the Secular World?

Chapter Preface

The Catholic Church has had a complex and often tumultuous history with the secular world, particularly in the areas of science and politics. In the twenty-first century, some factions of Catholics believe it is the church's holy mission to assert its values into the secular sphere, while nonbelievers and even other groups of Catholics hold that the church has no right to fashion itself into a conduit for political change. No matter how the world population has felt about the church's past and current commentary on nonreligious affairs, Catholicism has nonetheless offered its opinion on a wide range of such issues.

One of the church's most famous spars with science took place in the early 1600s, as the scientific revolution and the Age of Enlightenment were just beginning in the West. In 1633 the Roman Inquisition, a sweeping, church-sanctioned tribunal movement that sought to arrest and silence anyone accused of spreading doctrine contrary to the teachings of Catholicism, tried the Italian astronomer Galileo Galilei for heresy.

Galileo had publicly affirmed the view of the Renaissance Polish astronomer Nicolaus Copernicus that the sun, not Earth, was the center of the known universe and that Earth revolved around it. The church, meanwhile, had long posited the opposite view, that because God created Earth, it must be the center of the universe, with all other celestial bodies orbiting it. The Inquisition convicted Galileo in his 1633 trial, and he was forced to retract his heliocentric view of the universe and live under house arrest until his death. In the year 2000, Pope John Paul II officially apologized to the memory of Galileo for the scientist's abuse at the hands of the church.

More than two hundred years after the Inquisition, the Catholic Church revealed itself as still slightly wary of new scientific developments when it offered no opinion on Charles Darwin's 1859 theory of evolution. The church retained its silence on the matter for the next hundred years, but by the papacy of John Paul II in the final quarter of the twentieth century, it had finally admitted to "theistic evolution," the idea that God created the universe and then allowed evolution to occur naturally.

In the modern age, much of the controversy the Catholic Church has generated around science and politics has been related to the issues of abortion and contraception. On pro-life grounds, the church has long opposed the practice of both, while an increasingly socially liberal world contends that the church remains rooted in a conservative past. Pope Paul VI officially condemned contraception in 1968; continuing this stance, Pope Benedict XVI drew harsh criticism after his 2009 visit to Africa, when he claimed that condoms would exacerbate, rather than help, the HIV/AIDS epidemic that was sweeping the continent.

After becoming head of the church in early 2013, Pope Francis altered Catholicism's view of numerous issues in science and politics. He spoke out in favor of evolution and stopping global warming while claiming that all nations of the world should care more deeply for their poor, homeless, and marginalized. Many commentators inside and outside the church claimed that these positions made Pope Francis's church a more modern one, though some still lamented the pope's adherence to traditional Catholic views on abortion and contraception.

The following chapter presents opposing viewpoints relating to the Catholic Church and its association with the secular world. Topics include whether the church should concern itself with politics at all, Pope Francis's involvement in diplomacy efforts between the United States and Cuba, Francis's support of combating climate change, and the pope's endorsement of the big bang theory and evolution.

> *"'A good Catholic doesn't meddle in politics.' That's not true. . . . A good Catholic meddles in politics, offering the best of himself—so that those who govern can govern."*

The Catholic Church Should Participate in Politics

Keith Fournier

In the following viewpoint, Keith Fournier argues that the Catholic Church and all its members are morally obligated to participate in secular politics. As all people live in the society of the world, he claims, all have a duty to attempt to improve it. The church, Fournier believes, is especially required to do this as it must support its words on aiding the poor and helpless with deeds that accomplish these ends. Fournier is a Catholic deacon and editor in chief of Catholic Online.

As you read, consider the following questions:

1. What does Fournier say is the origin and original meaning of the word "politics"?

2. What does Fournier say was Cardinal Joseph Ratzinger's term for the condition under which the world is living?

3. What does Fournier claim happens to nations when natural moral law does not inform positive law?

In his daily homily of September 16, 2013, Pope Francis used the account of the Roman centurion to dabble in politics. . . . He spoke to those in public office. He also addressed the question of whether Christians should participate in politics.

Using the Old Testament leader David as an example for political leaders he was blunt. He reminded them they must love the people whom they serve, noting "a leader who doesn't love cannot govern—at best they can discipline, they can give a little bit of order, but they can't govern. You can't govern without loving the people and without humility! And every man, every woman who has to take up the service of government, must ask themselves two questions:

'Do I love my people in order to serve them better? Am I humble and do I listen to everybody, to diverse opinions in order to choose the best path?' If you don't ask those questions, your governance will not be good. The man or woman who governs—who loves his people is a humble man or woman."

He also had words for those indifferent to politics or who simply blame political leaders for all our problems, "None of us can say, 'I have nothing to do with this, they govern.' No, no, I am responsible for their governance, and I have to do the best so that they govern well, and I have to do my best by participating in politics according to my ability. Politics, according to the social doctrine of the church, is one of the highest forms of charity, because it serves the common good. I cannot wash my hands, eh? We all have to give something!"

Finally, he used the expression which is part of the title of this article: "'A good Catholic doesn't meddle in politics.' That's not true. That is not a good path. A good Catholic meddles in politics, offering the best of himself—so that those who govern can govern. But what is the best that we can offer to those who govern? Prayer!

"That's what Paul says: 'Pray for all people, and for the king and for all in authority.' 'But Father, that person is wicked, he should go to hell. . . .' Pray for him, pray for her, that they can govern well, that they can love their people, that they can serve their people, that they can be humble. A Christian who does not pray for those who govern is not a good Christian! 'But Father, how will I pray for that person, a person who has problems. . . .' 'Pray that that person might convert!'"

A Catholic Mission

The culture is a component of the broader mission field of the church. Politics is a subset of culture. The word is derived from a Greek word, *polis*, which literally means "city" or "city-state." Just as there can be no disembodied spirituality worthy of the name Christian—because redemption involves the integrated human person, body, soul and spirit—there cannot be a disembodied understanding of the mission we have as members of a church called into the world.

Catholics are not anti-government. We reject the notion that the isolated individual is the measure of freedom. We begin with the family as the first mediating association and move out from there, always respecting the principle of subsidiarity. However, the vision of the human person as called to community is integral to good governance.

In addition, the church must be guaranteed the freedom to proclaim her message in word and deed—in every nation and in every culture. That is her mission. Her message and mission are not confined to the walls of a church building. St. Paul used his Roman citizenship to advance the preaching of the Gospel. We must use our American citizenship to do the same in the United States. . . .

Moral Relativism

We are living under what Cardinal Joseph Ratzinger (Pope Emeritus Benedict XVI) labeled a dictatorship of relativism. Relativism is a philosophy which says there is nothing objectively true.

When there are no objective moral truths—which can be known by all and form the basis of our common life—there is no basis for true and responsible freedom. Freedom can never be realized, nor can it flourish, unless it is exercised in reference to choosing what is true and pursuing what is good.

As a nation we have lost our moral compass. As a direct result we are losing the very meaning of freedom. There can be no good governance in a nation when its moral foundations are gone. When a society fails to recognize that persons are more important than things it devolves into practical materialism.

The political leaders of our nation may still use the language of human rights, but the words have lost any moral content. Human rights do not exist in a vacuum; they are goods of the human person. When there is no recognition of a preeminent right to life, there soon follows an erosion of the entire structure of all human rights. We are at that stage, and we cannot sit idly by.

Failing to recognize that our first neighbors in the womb have a right to be born and live a full life as our neighbors in our community is the foundational failure we face as a nation. It is a rejection of our obligation in solidarity to one another. It denies the truth of being our brothers' (and sisters') keeper.

Catholic social teaching on the necessity of every nation giving a love of preference to the poor is rooted on our insistence that they have equal human dignity to everyone else, including children in the womb. Without the freedom to be born, all of the talk about compassion for the poor and the promotion of freedom throughout the entirety of life, and how we attain it, is hollow and empty. . . .

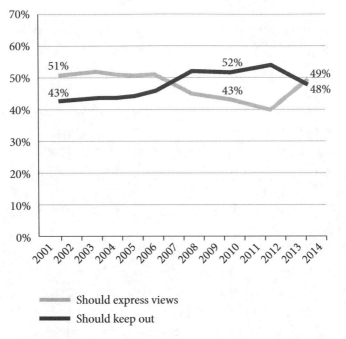

Growing Support for Religion in Politics

Should churches and other houses of worship keep out of political matters or express their views on day-to-day social and political questions?

Should express views

Should keep out

Survey conducted September 2–9, 2014. Don't know/refused responses not shown.

TAKEN FROM: "Public Sees Religion's Influence Waning," Pew Research Center, September 22, 2014.

A Moral Crisis

There is no solidarity in a culture that kills its own children and calls such evil a legal right. What we face in America is a moral crisis. Our leadership crisis flows directly from it. We cannot buy the lie that morally based positions are only "religious" and should be kept out of political discourse or campaigns. They are based upon the natural moral law which can be known by all men and women through the exercise of reason.

Acknowledgement of the existence of this natural moral law is the ground upon which every great civilization has been built. It is the source for every great and authentic human and civil rights movement. We honor Dr. Martin Luther King Jr. as a nation. We have a holiday which bears his name. He was a Christian minister and a heroic champion of human rights. His "Letter from Birmingham Jail" is an example of how reliance on the natural law is the ground of true freedom and necessary for a proper understanding of the source of our rights and the foundation of law itself. Dr. King wrote:

> "There are two types of laws: just and unjust. I would be the first to advocate obeying just laws. One has not only a legal but a moral responsibility to obey just laws. Conversely, one has a moral responsibility to disobey unjust laws. I would agree with St. Augustine that 'an unjust law is no law at all.'"...

Morality in Politics

Without the natural moral law informing the positive law, a nation devolves into anarchy. We need men and women to run for office and govern who are unafraid to acknowledge this fact and embrace a morally coherent approach to governing and public service. We need political parties to offer such morally coherent candidates for office.

The *Compendium of the Social Doctrine of the Church* says of political parties:

> Political parties have the task of fostering widespread participation and making public responsibilities accessible to all. Political parties are called to interpret the aspirations of civil society, orienting them towards the common good, offering citizens the effective possibility of contributing to the formulation of political choices. They must be democratic in their internal structure, and capable of political synthesis and planning.

I left the Democratic Party many years ago—after its leadership was taken over by the current morally incoherent coalition of social and cultural engineers which control it. I am now concerned about the leadership of the Republican Party. It is retreating from defending the moral foundations of a free society. . . .

There is a moral basis to every political and social concern, including economics. I now believe the Republican Party is at a new crossroad. What is needed is a new Republican Party with morally coherent candidates. I would also welcome a new Democratic Party.

It would be wonderful if both major political parties in this nation began with a bedrock commitment to the dignity of every human person from conception to natural death; the primacy of marriage and the family. . . ; a commitment to authentic human freedom (one which recognizes that it is not only a freedom from but also a freedom for and that true freedom is only realized when its exercise is directed toward what is good and true); and a commitment to solidarity as properly expressed through subsidiarity.

Then we could have a robust and healthy discussion on the size and role of government outside of the family and the role of mediating associations in good governance, the proper role of the nation in being a neighbor internationally, the proper understanding of a free economy as ordered toward promoting the freedom of the person and the common good . . . and many other vital political concerns.

A Catholic Duty

The collapse of Western civilization will not be remedied by political movements. They are inadequate for the task. The West has been seduced by the siren song of evil. However, we also must not withdraw from political participation. Catholics MUST meddle in politics. At the end of the *Catechism of the*

Catholic Church is a glossary. The term "human person" is followed with this description with which I conclude:

> PERSON, HUMAN: The human individual, made in the image of God; not something but someone, a unity of spirit and matter, soul and body, capable of knowledge, self-possession, and freedom, who can enter into communion with other persons—and with God. . . . The human person needs to live in society, which is a group of persons bound together organically by a principle of unity that goes beyond each one of them. . . .

Pope Francis Is Correct: A Good Catholic Meddles in Politics. With the . . . elections around the corner, it is time to commence the meddling.

> "The modern papacy has become as much a media institution as an ecclesiastical one."

How Pope Francis Allows Politics to Distort the Christian Faith

Michael Brendan Dougherty

In the following viewpoint, Michael Brendan Dougherty argues that Pope Francis should not guide the Catholic Church into politics. In doing so, Dougherty says, Francis has transformed certain actions that the church formerly recognized as personal sins and turned them into political choices, thus depleting them of moral import. Ultimately, Dougherty claims, a pope's personal interest in politics should not inform new church doctrine. Dougherty is senior correspondent at the Week.

As you read, consider the following questions:

1. What does Dougherty say Pope Francis called the Philippines' effort to legitimize the use of artificial contraception?

2. What does Dougherty say was Pope Paul VI's defense of the Catholic Church's refusal to alter its position on contraception in the encyclical *Humanae Vitae?*

3. What Catholic-themed novel does Dougherty say Pope Francis has continually referred to in his papacy?

Everyone seems to agree that Pope Francis is a unique figure. We're told he is humble. He's the "cool pope," unlike his predecessor Benedict. He is "earthy" and creative in his insults. Some Catholics, even my friends, think he is uniquely pastoral and personable. Others, like myself, find him uniquely opaque and exasperating.

That lack of clarity is partially attributable to Francis's fascination with politics. After the United States agreed to restore relations with Cuba, a deal that included the involvement of the pontiff himself, the Vatican's secretary of state emphasized Francis's ambitions for making the Holy See a bigger player in international diplomacy.

But it goes deeper than that. Politics and political metaphors shape his view of the world.

Francis's most recent comments in Manila [in the Philippines] affirming the church's ban on artificial contraception, as well as his later comment that Catholics are under no obligation to reproduce "like rabbits," were shaped by a political frame. You might even say his view is distorted by politics.

Before his now infamous "rabbits" comment, Francis described the effort to legitimate the use of artificial contraception in the Philippines as "ideological colonization." It reminded careful listeners of John Paul II's phrase "contraceptive imperialism," used to describe the way NGOs and other aid organizations premised aid on the acceptance and promotion of condoms or birth control pills.

In his interview, Francis said:

[Pope] Paul VI's rejection [of contraception] was not just in reference to individual cases: he told confessors to be understanding and merciful. He was looking at a universal neo-Malthusianism which was calling on world powers to control birth rates: births in Italy dropped to less than 1 percent and the same in Spain. [*Vatican Insider*]

In Manila, the pope used similar language:

Just as our peoples, at a certain moment of their history, were mature enough to say "no" to all forms of political colonization, so too in our families we need to be very wise, very shrewd, very strong, in order to say "no" to all attempts at an ideological colonization of our families. [*Vatican Insider*]

As history, this is an expansive reading of events. Of course there were disciples of Malthus warning of overpopulation in the 1960s. But internally, Paul VI was faced with a panel of experts that he himself had convened, who asked if he could find some way to lift the ban, couching it in the same pro-family, pro-responsibility, "under limited circumstances" rhetoric that accompanied a repeal of the contraception ban in the Anglican church at the Lambeth Conference in 1931. Pope Paul's response in the encyclical *Humanae Vitae* was not particularly political. Rather, it affirmed that he and the church had no right to change the laws of God, then dwelled on the beauty and consolations of that teaching, and the possible consequences of not following it.

For a man who issues such colorful and memorable put-downs, it's an odd tic of Francis's to retreat into political formulas to describe what the church once understood in terms of personal sin. Francis seems less horrified by mortal sin than by Americanization. I'm sure he would clarify, if it were put to him that way. But it reveals an instinct.

Retreating into politics is comfortable for Jesuits of a certain age. Reducing or transmuting Christian liturgy, theology, and scripture into politically ideological terms (or saying that these artifacts of the faith can only be understood in such terms) is not unique to Francis or even the modern period. It has roots going back six centuries.

Francis's determination to "make a mess," his loquacity, and political instincts have a disorienting effect. They exacerbate the fact that the modern papacy has become as much a media institution as an ecclesiastical one. It gives the impression that the Christian religion is a series of policies, many of which the pope has the power to change. It gives aid to those confused theologians who think the historic dogmas and doctrines of the church are merely historically accidental "emphases" on this or that aspect of the Gospel. Revised doctrines could presumably give a different but still legitimate emphasis on the same. So why not let this popular pope do just that?

In these same recent interviews, Pope Francis referenced a 1903 novel by Robert Hugh Benson, *Lord of the World*, which he has brought up before. Benson's work is possibly the first ever dystopian novel. It's about a Catholic apocalypse, treasured by some traditional Catholics. It's the story of the anti-Christ taking power and restoring all peace to Europe through a universal dictatorship, which eventually sets out to exterminate the remnants of the church after a new, misguided gunpowder plot.

The protagonist eventually becomes a pope of an underground church. He mostly lives alone and in secret in the Middle East, offering the Mass and governing the remnant church through secret private messages sent out to individual bishops.

It is fascinating that Pope Francis keeps recommending this book to people, precisely because that fictive papacy is the very opposite of his: unpopular, feared, hated, and marginalized. It is entirely transfixed with Masses done in private, to please God and to reconcile the world to him. He faithfully recites the words handed onto him. He prays, and encourages.

It would be possible for a pope to imitate that example today from a Vatican palace. The pope would give only small private audiences, and trust other cardinals to give sermons at his public liturgies. His words would still govern and appoint, but from behind closed doors. But he would (and should) avoid Pope Benedict's practice of publishing books while pope. He would extinguish Francis's habit of extemporaneous speech. It would be a truly humble papacy, where politics is avoided, and where the personality of the occupant does not presage some reform. A servant of the servants.

One can hope.

> "[Pope Francis] brokered a new day for relations between the United States and Cuba, and the leaders of both nations publicly thanked him for his efforts."

Pope Francis Is Correct on New American-Cuban Relations

William R. Wineke

In the following viewpoint, William R. Wineke argues that Pope Francis rightly brokered the political deal between the United States and Cuba that restored full diplomatic ties between the two countries for the first time in more than fifty years. Wineke claims that Francis was able to do so because he does not totally support either American capitalism or Cuban communism. More importantly, Wineke claims, Pope Francis's aid in the deal shows only that he was interested in helping end a pointless political stalemate. Wineke is a journalist for the Channel 3000 news network in Madison, Wisconsin.

As you read, consider the following questions:

1. How does Wineke say loyal Catholics describe Pope Francis?

2. What importance does Wineke say loyal Catholics and would-be Catholic spokespeople assign to Pope John Paul II regarding the end of the Cold War?

3. What three helpful changes does Wineke say Pope Francis can make by his popularity?

It looks to me as if Pope Francis will have a happy Christmas.

He just turned 78 years old and still has a job. That's inspirational for those of us who really don't do well with the idea of retirement.

He brokered a new day for relations between the United States and Cuba, and the leaders of both nations publicly thanked him for his efforts. That has to be good news for the church. When you hear the word "Catholic" today, you are more likely to think of this charismatic pope than you are to conjure up images of predator priests.

And he observed his birthday by handing out 400 sleeping bags to the homeless in Rome. Each carries a papal insignia, which probably means most of them will be sold. So what?

An Outdated View

Predictably, Catholic conservatives (I really hate to use that term for reactionaries whose goal is to put Christ in a doctrinal box and keep him there, but I don't know any better term to use) are apoplectic.

They present the pope, at best, as a naive, meddling old man whose worldview is warped by his history as a Latin American priest and who doesn't understand that the Cuban regime is Communist and, therefore, evil.

Those are the folks who are loyal Catholics and believe the pope is the legitimate successor to St. Peter, just a bit misguided. There are also would-be Catholic spokespeople who think Francis is the anti-pope and that Pope Benedict should give up his retirement and return to the papal throne.

Pope "Pivotal" in US-Cuban Diplomacy

One thing is certain about Pope Francis's visit to Cuba in September [2015]: He is going to be welcomed with open arms.

"He will receive the warmest hospitality of the Cuban people," the island's foreign minister, Bruno Rodríguez Parrilla, said on Wednesday [in April 2015].

It couldn't be any other way. After all, Francis played a pivotal role in creating the conditions for a new relationship between Cuba and the United States, after more than half a century of enmity and distrust.

His visit to the island before heading for the U.S will come at a time of unprecedented change and hope for the Cuban people and is sure to give a boost to the conversations between the two nations. As Rodríguez Parrilla said, Francis's visit will be "memorable."

"This pope has worked to make reconciliation possible. The fact that he is going to Cuba before traveling to the U.S. is significant," said Julio Ruiz, a Cuban-American geriatric psychiatrist and a proponent of a more rational U.S.-Cuba policy.

Francis will be the third pope to visit Cuba in less than 20 years, something that Ruiz, who defines himself as nonreligious, says is "almost a miracle."

Albor Ruiz,
"Cuban Leaders Are Prepared to Show Pope Francis Their
'Warmest Hospitality' When He Visits the Island in September,"
New York Daily News, *April 27, 2015.*

What they have in common is that each group seems to believe that there continues to be a war to the death between

Catholicism and communism. Ironically, one of their heroes is Pope John Paul II, whom they rightly credit for having contributed to the end of the Cold War [political tension between the United States and the Soviet Union that started after 1945 and lasted until 1991] and the defeat of international communism, but whom they forget also tried to build better ties between the Vatican and Marxist governments.

Pope of Symbols

The fact is that the Vatican has never endorsed the unfettered capitalism that American economic nihilists find so romantic. Nor is Pope Francis the naive liberal that so many American Catholics find so appealing and so many American conservatives find frightening.

What he does understand better than most of his predecessors is the value of the symbol.

He can kiss a baby, embrace a leper, give away 400 sleeping bags and ride around town in a Fiat and be guaranteed positive front-page news.

With the popularity he gains by these gestures, he can warn the church against clericalism, take charge of a chaotic and often corrupt financial system in the Vatican and use the moral authority of his office to help end a 50-year cold war between the United States and Cuba, a war that accomplished absolutely nothing except impoverishing the Cuban people.

Symbols are important. Jesus was born in Bethlehem in a stable lying in a manger. We all know that story. We remember it today.

No one remembers where King Herod was born and no one cares.

Pope Francis isn't Jesus, but his papacy will be remembered long after those of some of his predecessors will be relegated to only the interest of scholars.

> "The pontiff seems to have blessed the Cuban opposition with one hand, and the Castro brothers with the other."

Cuban Dissident Voices and Pope Francis's Deaf Ears

Nicholas G. Hahn III

In the following viewpoint, Nicholas G. Hahn III argues that Pope Francis settled for a bad deal between the United States and Cuba. A better deal, Hahn claims, would have seen the pope holding out for certain concessions from the Communist Cuban government, such as a transformation to democracy. In Hahn's view, Pope Francis, as a Latin American who has experienced political repression, should have known that the Cuban people truly desired freedom. Hahn is the editor of RealClearReligion .org.

As you read, consider the following questions:

1. According to Hahn, what do some Cuban dissident groups say would result from increased American trade with Cuba?

2. For what aspects of the United States–Cuba deal does Hahn say Senator Marco Rubio blamed both President Barack Obama and Pope Francis?

3. During what era in Argentina does Hahn say Pope Francis was head of the Jesuits?

When Berta Soler met Pope Francis, it had been a long time coming.

Soler's Ladies in White, a Catholic opposition movement comprised of relatives of jailed human rights activists in Cuba, had pleaded numerous times for a meeting with Pope Benedict XVI. He declined and visited the Communist island in 2012 only to continue a policy of détente established by his predecessor, John Paul II.

But a short blessing by Pope Francis in March 2013 signaled a slight shift in direction—or that's at least what Soler believed.

"We think a Latin American pope is very good for us. Pope Francis knows a little better the problems that our peoples have, he comes from far down and he can help the people who are suffering," Soler told the Italian newspaper *La Stampa* after receiving some papal encouragement.

If only Soler and her Ladies had known better. Last week [in December 2014], the Vatican confirmed that for more than 18 months, the Holy See had been working to restore diplomatic relations between the United States and Cuba. The pontiff seems to have blessed the Cuban opposition with one hand, and the Castro brothers [referring to Cuban dictators Raúl and Fidel Castro] with the other.

Soler's Ladies, Cuban exiles, and other dissident groups have long lobbied against new relations without any concessions from the Communist regime. They aren't as hopeful as others who say more U.S. trade with the Caribbean island may lead to more freedom.

The international aid worker Alan Gross's release is perhaps the only Cuban concession—and thank goodness for that—but even so, it came as a small part of a lopsided prisoner swap.

"Democracy and freedom for the Cuban people aren't going to be achieved by what Obama has given to the Cuban government," Soler said in a post on her group's website. In his announcement of reestablishing diplomatic relations, President [Barack] Obama thanked Pope Francis for helping broker a Cold War–era [referring to the period of political tension between the United States and the Soviet Union that started after 1945 and lasted until 1991] thawing, saying his "moral example shows us the importance of pursuing the world as it should be, rather than simply settling for the world as it is."

The president and the pope may be settling for far less than they might think. Sen. Marco Rubio, a Catholic and son of parents who fled the Communist paradise, denounced, warning that the move as "more than just putting U.S. national security at risk, President Obama is letting down the Cuban people, who still yearn to be free." Rubio didn't spare any words for his spiritual shepherd, who he politely encouraged to "take up the cause of freedom and democracy, which is critical for a free people—for a people to truly be free."

The Argentine pontiff should know a thing or two about the church's cause for freedom. When a military junta in his own country took power in a 1976 coup during what is called the "Dirty War," Father Bergoglio was head of the Jesuits.

The future Pope saw many of his priests and seminarians jailed and killed. Bergoglio is reported to have helped many flee the country and even met with the military dictatorship to save the lives of two imprisoned priests.

But those experiences may not have been on the pontiff's mind when he wrote personal letters to Obama and [Raúl] Castro or when he hosted delegates from Cuba at the Vatican.

While it might be fodder for sensational journalism, Rubio and other Catholics who make public policy shouldn't have to correct their pontiff on foreign affairs. Clerics are spiritual leaders, not political ones. When prelates pretend to be diplomats, it dilutes their authority on issues of faith and morals.

Francis might have done one better by prodding the Castro brothers about their regime's woeful human rights record. That would have been in a pope's wheelhouse.

And it would have been what Berta Soler deserved.

> *"If Pope Francis embraces the climate change agenda, he will be aligning himself with the biggest enemies of the church and of Catholic moral principles."*

Pope Francis Is Wrong to Combat Climate Change

Marc Morano

In the following viewpoint, Marc Morano argues that Pope Francis is misinformed in his endeavor to combat climate change. Fossil fuels have helped to save the lives of the poor, Morano claims, and all signs of global warming are receding. In Morano's view, Pope Francis is wrongfully allying himself with radical climate change activists who will lead him further into mistaken science. Morano is editor of the Climate Depot website.

As you read, consider the following questions:

1. What does Morano say will result from the continued development of fossil fuels?

2. What aspects of the global warming narrative does Morano say have weakened?

Marc Morano, "Pope Francis Is Misguided on Climate Change," Spero News, January 15, 2015. speroforum.com. Copyright © 2015 Spero News. All rights reserved. Reproduced with permission.

3. What various anti-Catholic stances does Morano say
   climate change agenda supporters take?

The pope's claim that "It is man who has slapped nature in
the face" needs to be weighed against the fact that fossil
fuels have allowed mankind to stop nature from slapping man
in the face. The more we develop with fossil fuels and increase
our wealth and standard of living, the more we can inoculate
ourselves from the ravages of nature.

That is why fossil fuel use is the moral choice to make.
Sadly, the pope is aligning himself with a corrupt UN [United
Nations] agenda that will limit development for billions of the
world's desperately poor residents.

Pope Misled on Science

If Pope Francis goes ahead with his climate encyclical and
uses it to essentially lobby nations to commit to a
development-limiting UN climate treaty, it will be unprecedented action and massively misguided.

The pope has been misled on climate science and his promotion of the UN agenda will only mean the poor will be the
biggest victims of climate change policies. The pope has picked
a contentious scientific issue in which—now going on almost
two decades of no global warming, sea ice recovering, sea level
rise actually decelerating, on every metric from polar bears on
down—the global warming narrative has weakened. And to
now have the pope jump on that bandwagon would sow confusion among Catholics.

If Pope Francis embraces the climate change agenda, he
will be aligning himself with the biggest enemies of the church
and of Catholic moral principles. These activists are pro-
population control, pro-abortion, pro-contraception, pro-
sterilization, pro-euthanasia, etc. Some climate activists have
even called for genetically altering humans to fight global
warming.

What is Pope Francis thinking? How could he be so off course on climate?

Bad Advice

The advocates of the climate change narrative see humans as the biggest threat to the planet, as opposed to the Catholic view that the planet exists to sustain us, not the other way around. The moral principle of good stewardship is rooted in the idea that creation is a gift to us from God.

Development is needed for so much of the world, and carbon-based energy is one of the greatest liberators of mankind, lengthening life expectancy, lowering infant mortality and bringing running water and electricity to those who need it most.

The Vatican is taking advice from the hard-core climate activists who specialize in extreme rants. A workshop of the Pontifical Academy of Sciences held in 2014 was reportedly a key influence on the pope's views. The proceedings of the workshop included activists like Naomi Oreskes, Peter Wadhams, Martin Rees, Hans Joachim Schellnhuber, Jeffrey Sachs and Joseph Stiglitz.

One of the attendees was Jeffrey Sachs, a UN special advisor [to] UN secretary-general Ban Ki-moon. Sachs tweeted on November 10 that "Climate liars like Rupert Murdoch & Koch brothers [billionaire brothers Charles and David Koch] have more & more blood on their hands as climate disasters claim lives across the world."

The pope is taking advice from Sachs?

Peter Wadhams is a scientist that even his fellow global warming advocates distance themselves from.

German climate advisor Hans Joachim Schellnhuber was also at the Vatican climate presentation in 2014. Does Pope Francis want to align himself with Schellnhuber's views?

Naomi Oreskes is known for advocating climate skeptics who dissent from the UN/[Al] Gore climate alarmist view be prosecuted as mobsters!

An Education

Pope Francis needs to hear from the scientists who reject the man-made global warming narrative that has been manufactured by the UN, Al Gore and the media. And I am willing to organize a counter-meeting of dissenting scientists to make a presentation to the Pontifical Academy of Sciences.

The pope needs to educate himself on climate science and the agenda of climate activists.

"*It is beyond high time for the world, and 'all Catholics' to join the fight to reduce the existential threat to human beings from anthropogenic climate change.*"

Pope Francis Displays Sound Ethics in Combating Climate Change

Rmuse

In the following viewpoint, Rmuse argues that Pope Francis is performing the good work of Jesus Christ by advocating for solutions to climate change. Rmuse agrees with the pope that sins against Earth are sins against humanity. Rmuse contends, however, that although Pope Francis is ethical in his fight, he will continue to encounter resistance from various religious and political factions who profit from fossil fuels. Rmuse is a former minister and a writer for PoliticusUSA.com as well as numerous other outlets.

As you read, consider the following questions:

1. From what three groups does Rmuse say Pope Francis has encountered opposition in his effort to combat climate change?

2. What two labels does Rmuse say the Cornwall Alliance for the Stewardship of Creation assigned to the American environmental movement?

3. What does Rmuse say angers Republicans, the religious right, and the Koch brothers about Pope Francis?

One of the greatest things to happen over the past year is the remarkable revelation that there is finally, at long last, a major Christian leader, and member of the clergy, who espouses, embraces, and promotes the teachings of Jesus Christ. Even for an avowed secular humanist, this is a stunning, and welcomed, development if for no other reason than one of the world's leading religions appears to be adopting Christ's regard for the world's poor and downtrodden. Of course, the Catholic pope has garnered nothing but serious opposition and pushback from America's evangelical and Catholic Republican movement, and now the Koch brothers [referring to billionaire brothers Charles and David Koch] and their dirty energy cabal have joined what is developing into a dirty oil–evangelical war against Pope Francis.

The Pope's Enemies

The pope already drew the wrath of both evangelical and Catholic Republicans in Congress for criticizing the greed and income inequality championed by the GOP, but now he has the undivided attention of the Koch brothers, Exxon, and their dirty energy cohorts. The cause célèbre for the Koch-funded evangelical movement is the pope's recent announcement that it is beyond high time for the world, and "all Catholics" to join the fight to reduce the existential threat to human beings from anthropogenic climate change. Last October [2014], the pope harshly condemned "the monopolizing of lands, deforestation, the appropriation of water, inadequate agro-toxics that are some of the evils that tear man from the land of his birth. Climate change, the loss of biodiversity and deforestation are already showing their devastating effects in the great cataclysms we witness."

Those words, although accurate, were toxic to a Koch-funded evangelical Christian group made up of pastors and Christian leaders, the Cornwall Alliance [for the Stewardship of Creation], that considers the devastating effects and great cataclysms we witness from the effects of anthropogenic (man-made) climate change the will of almighty God and biblical. A godly will that no man, much less the Vicar of Christ, dares speak out against or attempt to change. In the view of evangelicals and their leaders, if man destroys the environment and threatens human existence, it is God's will and they will fight to see climate change's full effects to fruition; for God, the Bible, and the mountains of cash from the Koch brothers' dirty energy cabal. Besides, evangelicals could not care one iota less if Earth becomes uninhabitable because something about an absurd idea of being "raptured" away for a ringside seat as those sinners "left behind" receive God's almighty wrath in the war of Armageddon.

The Cornwall Alliance was quick to lash out at the pope this week when he announced he would be issuing a "rare encyclical on the environment and climate change" early this year [2015], as well as convene a summit of the world's religious leaders to address climate change. Pope Francis will also address the United Nations [UN] General Assembly with a view toward influencing the upcoming UN meeting on climate change in Paris this year.

Evangelical Opposition

The pope's announcement drew a harsh rebuke from the religious right's Cornwall Alliance, whose spokesman, [E.] Calvin Beisner, said that regardless of his position as pope, or intent to help mankind, "Francis will be opposed by the powerful US evangelical movement." The Koch-funded Cornwall Alliance for the Stewardship of Creation had previously issued a bibli-

Pope Francis Pushes Environmental Campaign

Since his first homily in 2013, Pope Francis has preached about the need to protect the earth and all of creation as part of a broad message on the environment. It has caused little controversy so far.

But now, as Francis prepares to deliver what is likely to be a highly influential encyclical this summer [in 2015] on environmental degradation and the effects of human-caused climate change on the poor, he is alarming some conservatives in the United States who are loath to see the Catholic Church reposition itself as a mighty voice in a cause they do not believe in. . . .

Francis's policy moves on climate change, particularly his use of the encyclical, go far beyond what has come before. Catholics point to other papal encyclicals that have had public policy impacts: Pope Leo XIII's 1891 encyclical on labor and workers' rights is believed to have spurred the workers' rights movement and led to the creation of labor unions. . . .

Francis, who chose the name of St. Francis of Assisi, the patron saint of animals and the environment, has had far more influence on the church and public. . . . He has been embraced for his humility, antipoverty agenda, progressive statements on social issues and efforts to reform the Vatican bureaucracy.

This month he said in a Twitter post: "We need to care for the earth so that it may continue, as God willed, to be a source of life for the entire human family."

Coral Davenport and Laurie Goodstein,
"Pope Francis Steps Up Campaign on Climate Change, to
Conservatives' Alarm," New York Times, April 27, 2015.

cal declaration labeling the American environmental movement a dirty false religion and "unbiblical." There is nothing whatsoever in any version of the Christian Bible that refers to the American environmental movement as a religion, false or otherwise, or contrary to biblical principles. But American evangelicals cannot be expected to know the contents of an alleged holy book they refuse to read much less follow.

Beisner also warned the pope that he had better "back off" talking about combatting climate change saying that although "the Catholic church is correct on ethical principles, it has been misled on science. It follows that the policies the Vatican is promoting are incorrect. Our position reflects the views of millions of evangelical Christians in the US" as well as the Koch brothers who fund the Cornwall Alliance. In fact, as an evangelical group, "specializing in promoting pollution" has been a funding bonanza for the evangelicals who issued their own Christian edict that "to believe in climate change is really an insult to God and will lead to tyranny." Leave it to American-style bastardized Christianity to know what their god considers an insult; unless their "god" is the Koch brothers' dirty energy industry money.

There are some addressable issues in Beisner's warning to Jesus Christ's "representative on Earth" to back off and stay out of the fossil fuel industry's business of decimating the environment. The only "ethical principle" evangelicals agree with Catholic doctrine on is controlling women by banning all forms of "unnatural birth control." Other than that one abominable concurrence, this new pope's adherence to the biblical Jesus Christ's teachings that "millions of evangelical Christians" reject is a major source of angst and ire to Republicans, the religious right, and their funding machine the Koch brothers. That the Pope embraces the obvious science and empirical truth about anthropogenic climate change, and is joining the battle to assuage its destruction, is why the Kochs and their dirty energy cabal are funding the evangelical war against the pope; to perpetuate the damage from climate change and their ungodly profits.

The Coming Stalemate

This is not Cornwall's first foray into the war to increase carbon emissions and oil industry profits. A couple of years ago one of the Kochs' and oil industry's greatest political and legislative arms, the Heritage Foundation, gave the evangelical Cornwall organization a forum to roll out its crusade against climate science called "Resisting the Green Dragon." According to Cornwall's pastors and Christian leaders, the Kochs' oil industry campaign against efforts to combat climate change is the evangelical movement's "biblical response to one of the greatest deceptions of our day" against what they have labeled "a false religion." The group claims the entire climate change movement is a "nefarious conspiracy to empower eugenicists and create a global government" and portrays even the idea of climate change as the work of Satan the Devil.

Pope Francis has already shown he is not swayed, impressed, or intimidated by evangelical or Catholic Republicans in Congress so it is highly unlikely he will be terrorized by "millions of American evangelical Christians" or their Koch brother, filthy energy industry funding machine. The relationship between the Kochs and Cornwall is symbiotic in that the Kochs get a ready-made batch of religious sycophants dedicated to supporting the destruction of the environment to hasten the onset of their cherished end time "rapture," and the Cornwall Alliance evangelical pastors and leaders get an endless supply of Koch, Exxon, and oil industry cash.

The pope may not be an environmental champion yet, especially in America, but because he is the first pope in generations to actually espouse the teachings of Jesus Christ, it is highly likely his war on global climate change will garner widespread support from the estimated 1.2 billion Catholic devotees around the world. Still, with only millions of American "onward Christian soldiers" in the evangelical movement opposing the pope, and unlimited Koch and oil industry money, one can only assume that the Koch war on the pope will not end quickly; at least not in America.

> *"Pope Francis has compromised biblical authority in favor of man's ideas in the area of origins."*

Pope Francis Is Wrong to Support Big Bang and Evolution

Ken Ham

In the following viewpoint, Ken Ham argues that Pope Francis has wrongly replaced God's word with man's word by claiming that the big bang theory and evolution are compatible with God's creation. The pope is also incorrect, Ham contends, in believing that God's word changes over time, for this would imply that God's word was not perfect. In Ham's view, Pope Francis has misinterpreted the Bible by holding that some aspects of the universe are out of God's control. Ham is the founder and president of Answers in Genesis, a Christian organization.

As you read, consider the following questions:

1. What examples does Ham provide of the ways in which the God of the scripture can make anything?

Ken Ham, "Is the Pope Right That 'God Is Not Afraid of New Things'?," *Answers in Genesis* (blog), October 29, 2014. http://blogs.answersingenesis.org. Copyright © 2014 Answers in Genesis. All rights reserved. Reproduced with permission.

2. To what two other social issues does Ham say Pope Francis is attempting to apply his skewed view of God's word?

3. What untruth from the Bible does Ham say is rehashed in Pope Francis's attempt to place man's word over God's?

Pope Francis is not the first religious leader who has endorsed evolution and the big bang, but he is certainly one of the most influential.

Following in the tradition of other recent popes, Pope Francis has compromised biblical authority in favor of man's ideas in the area of origins. He said, "The big bang, that today is considered to be the origin of the world, does not contradict the creative intervention of God; on the contrary, it requires it. Evolution in nature is not in contrast with the notion of [divine] creation because evolution requires the creation of the beings that evolve."

About the account of creation in Genesis, the pope stated, "When we read about creation in Genesis, we run the risk of imagining God was a magician, with a magic wand able to do everything. But that is not so . . . God is not a divine being or a magician, but the Creator who brought everything to life . . . Evolution in nature is not inconsistent with the notion of creation, because evolution requires the creation of beings that evolve." Additionally, Pope Francis said that "God is not afraid of new things."

Now, of course God is not a "magician." Nothing in scripture ever hints that He is—especially not in the creation account. Scripture portrays God as the all-powerful Creator who is capable of making anything, whether that's creating the universe out of nothing, parting the Red Sea, saving people from a fiery furnace, walking on water, or raising the dead! God even says the following:

Big Bang Theory Conceived by Catholic Priest

Atheists, devout Christians, you might want to sit down for this: The big bang theory was first proposed by a Roman Catholic priest.

It wasn't just any priest. It was Monseigneur George Lemaître, a brilliant Belgian who entered the priesthood following his service as an artillery officer in the Belgian army during World War I. He was also an accomplished astronomer and a talented mathematician and physician. . . .

In the late 1920s, Lemaître quietly put forth a theory he called his "hypothesis of the primeval atom. . . ."

Lemaître imagined that if the universe was expanding, it had to be expanding from somewhere and some point in time. He figured that if you traced the idea of the universe back in time, all the way to the very beginning, everything had to converge into a single point. Lemaître called that point a super-atom. He suggested that the expansion of the universe had resulted from the explosion of this super-atom that hurled materials in all directions, and set the universe as we know it in motion. . . .

As astonishing as Lemaître's idea was, perhaps equally surprising to us now was the reaction of the church. . . . In the early 1950s, Pope Pius XII not only declared that the big bang and the Catholic concept of creation were compatible; he embraced Lemaître's idea as scientific validation for the existence of God and of Catholicism.

Edgar B. Herwick,
"Big Bang Theory: A Roman Catholic Creation,"
WGBH News, March 20, 2014.

Behold, I am the LORD, the God of all flesh. Is there anything too hard for Me? (Jeremiah 32:27)

The Unchangeable God

Because God created nature and natural laws, He alone has power over them. The God of scripture who can do anything (Job 42:2; Matthew 19:26) is absolutely able to create out of nothing, just as He said He did: "By faith we understand that the worlds were framed by the word of God, so that the things which are seen were not made of things which are visible" (Hebrews 11:3). And most importantly, God does not change (James 1:17).

In this instance, Pope Francis, like so many other religious leaders, is putting man's word above God's word. And not only that, he's also going so far as to say that only a magician with "a magic wand" could create the way that God said He created in Genesis! Frankly, this shows a lack of understanding of who scripture claims God is—the all-powerful Creator (Isaiah 44:24) who is capable of doing what is impossible to man (Matthew 19:26). Sadly, this view of God is rapidly spreading even throughout the Protestant church.

A statement made by the pope earlier this month at a conference about homosexuality and divorce further shows how this leader views God and His word: "God is not afraid of new things." What the pope and many other religious leaders are saying is that God—and His word—is open to change as society's opinions change. But is this what God's word teaches? Absolutely not. In His word, God says, "I am the Lord, I do not change" (Malachi 3:6) and "God is not a man, that He should lie, nor a son of man, that He should repent. Has He said, and will He not do? Or has He spoken, and will He not make it good?" (Numbers 23:19). Of scripture, God says, "Heaven and earth will pass away, but My words will by no means pass away" (Matthew 24:35) and "The grass withers, the flower fades, but the word of our God stands forever" (Isaiah 40:8).

God and His word are not open to arbitrary change simply because society changes as it is influenced by false religions. God's word "endures forever" (1 Peter 1:25) and is "profitable for doctrine, for reproof, for correction, for instruction in righteousness" (2 Timothy 3:16) regardless of the generation.

Man Against God

Think about it: If God and His word are open to change, then God's word is not an authority on anything—man becomes the authority because he gets to decide when and how God's word applies. This is simply a recycling of the same old lie from the Garden of Eden, "Has God really said . . . ?" (Genesis 3:1, NIV [New International Version]). Sadly, religious leaders all around the world are falling for this lie and choosing to reinterpret God's word based on man's fallible ideas. By and large, God is not the authority anymore—sinful man is. But it is God's word—not man's word—that is truth (John 17:17).

I encourage you to pray that church leaders like these will realize that they are placing man's opinions above God's word and that they will repent and trust God's word, beginning in Genesis.

| "*Early philosophers . . . all felt nature's wonder and beauty reflected the beauty and perfection of their maker.*"

Pope Francis's Big Bang and Evolution Support Aligns with Catholicism

Thomas Lucente

In the following viewpoint, Thomas Lucente argues that Pope Francis's assertions that the big bang theory and evolution are true are not unusual in the Catholic Church. Lucente supports his argument by claiming that Francis, like many great Christian thinkers of the past, has used reason to decipher God's creation. Reason, Lucente contends, complements faith, and in utilizing both, Pope Francis is carrying on a Christian tradition of explaining the universe. Lucente is an Ohio attorney and an editor of Lima News.

As you read, consider the following questions:

1. How does Lucente say Justin Martyr referred to Plato?

2. According to Lucente, in what ways did Martyr say Greek philosophy and Christianity were similar?

3. As stated by Lucente, how does Rafael Vicuna say Plato, St. Thomas Aquinas, and St. Augustine felt about nature's wonder and beauty?

Pope Francis made headlines last week [in October 2014] by simply stating the obvious.

In a speech to the Pontifical Academy of Sciences on Monday, the pontiff said: "The big bang, which today is held as the beginning of the world, does not contradict the intervention of the divine creator, but requires it. Evolution in nature is not at odds with the notion of creation because evolution presupposes the creation of beings that evolve."

Restating Tradition

The pope's comments denouncing a literal interpretation of the creation account found in Genesis is a long-standing church position dating to the earliest days of Christianity.

The church fathers were followers of the Platonic [relating to Greek philosopher and mathematician Plato] commitment to reason. This is evidenced by early Christian writings.

Justin Martyr, a church leader who lived in the early part of the second century, said, "The Gospel and the best elements in Plato and the Stoics are almost identical ways of apprehending the same truth."

Because of this, he referred to Plato as a "Christian before Christ."

Justin pointed out that Greek philosophy and Christianity are similar because both rest on the divine gift of reason and that because this was God's greatest gift, then Christian revelation must be compatible with "the highest Reason."

It was in this vein that St. Augustine of Hippo, one of Christianity's greatest theologians, a man honored by Catholics and Protestants alike, including Lutherans, Anglicans and Calvinists, specifically rejected a literal view of creationism in the early fifth century.

In his exegetical commentaries on the Book of Genesis, the church father wrote: "In matters that are obscure and far beyond our vision, even in such as we may find treated in Holy Scripture, different interpretations are sometimes possible without prejudice to the faith we have received. In such a case, we should not rush in headlong and so firmly take our stand on one side that, if further progress in the search of truth justly undermines this position, we too fall with it."

Augustine cautioned Christians against using the Bible as a science book and taking a dogmatic approach to a literal interpretation of Genesis.

He criticized those who used scripture to contradict reason: "Reckless and incompetent expounders of Holy Scripture bring untold trouble and sorrow on their wiser brethren when they are caught in one of their mischievous false opinions and are taken to task by those who are not bound by the authority of our sacred books. For then, to defend their utterly foolish and obviously untrue statements, they will try to call upon Holy Scripture for proof and even recite from memory many passages which they think support their position, although they understand neither what they say nor the things about which they make assertion."

To Augustine, reason was indispensable to faith: "Heaven forbid that God should hate in us that by which he made us superior to the animals! Heaven forbid that we should believe in such a way as not to accept or seek reasons, since we could not even believe if we did not possess rational souls."

Indeed, faith without reason is but a rudderless ship.

Faith and Reason

Another speaker at the conference, Rafael Vicuña, professor of molecular genetics and molecular biology at the Pontifical Catholic University of Chile, said it would be a mistake for re-

Evolution and Big Bang Theory Do Not Push Aside God

The big bang theory and evolution do not eliminate the existence of God, who remains the one who set all of creation into motion, Pope Francis told his own science academy.

And God's existence does not contradict the discoveries of science, he told members of the Pontifical Academy of Sciences Oct. 27.

"When we read the account of creation in Genesis, we risk thinking that God was a magician, complete with a magic wand, able to do everything. But it is not like that," he said. "He created living beings and he let them develop according to the internal laws that he gave each one, so that they would develop and reach their full potential."

God gave creation full autonomy while also guaranteeing his constant presence in nature and people's lives, he said.

The beginning of the world is not a result of "chaos," he said, but comes directly from "a supreme principle that creates out of love."

Carol Glatz,
"Pope: Evolution, Big Bang Do Not Push Aside God,
Who Set It in Motion," Catholic News Service, October 28, 2014.

ligion to try to solve the mysteries in nature by making God "responsible for a natural process that escapes scientific explanation."

He pointed to the intelligent design movement and rejected its claims that God must have guided the development of evolution through the eons because of its complexity.

Not only are intelligent-design proponents "denying nature's autonomy, but they are also revealing some degree of ingenuousness, because science has already provided explanations for the development" of structures they had considered to be too complex to occur naturally, he said.

Early philosophers such as Plato, St. Thomas Aquinas and St. Augustine all felt nature's wonder and beauty reflected the beauty and perfection of their maker, Vicuña said.

So, when Francis told the academy the big bang theory and evolution do not eliminate the existence of God, he was not saying anything new or newsworthy. He was merely expressing centuries of Christian teaching and demonstrating that divine gift of reason.

Periodical and Internet Sources Bibliography

The following articles have been selected to supplement the diverse views presented in this chapter.

Michelle Boorstein	"Pope Francis Takes a Public Role in U.S.-Cuba Relations," *Washington Post*, December 17, 2014.
Elizabeth Dias	"Sorry, but Media Coverage of Pope Francis Is Papal Bull," *Time*, October 29, 2014.
Anthony Faiola, Michelle Boorstein, and Chris Mooney	"Release of Encyclical Reveals Pope's Deep Dive into Climate Science," *Washington Post*, June 18, 2015.
Christopher J. Hale	"The 5 Most Important Points of Pope Francis's Climate Change Encyclical," *Time*, June 18, 2015.
Miriam Krule	"Pope Francis' Progressive Statement on Evolution Is Not Actually a Departure for the Catholic Church," *Slate*, October 28, 2014.
Alexander Lucie-Smith	"Do We Really Need a Papal Encyclical on Climate Change?," *Catholic Herald*, January 2, 2015.
Josephine McKenna	"Pope Says Evolution, Big Bang Are Real," *USA Today*, October 28, 2014.
Michael O'Loughlin and Inés San Martín	"Pope Francis Helped Broker the Restoration of US-Cuban Relations," Crux, December 17, 2014.
Dan Roberts and Rory Carroll	"Obama and Raúl Castro Thank Pope for Breakthrough in US-Cuba Relations," *Guardian*, December 17, 2014.
Taylor Wofford	"Pope Francis's Remarks on Evolution Are Not That Controversial Among Roman Catholics," *Newsweek*, October 30, 2014.

For Further Discussion

Chapter 1

1. Francis DeBernardo argues that the Catholic Church's change in attitude toward gay people will eventually lead to a change in doctrine, hinting that the church has begun the process of accepting gay marriage. Do you think DeBernardo's logic is sound? Does a change in attitude always necessitate an eventual change in practice? Explain your reasoning.

2. John Zmirak contends that President Barack Obama's initiative to force Catholic institutions to hire openly gay employees persecutes the organizations by forcing them to act against their religious beliefs. Do you agree with Zmirak that religious freedom precludes granting equal rights to all aspiring workers? Explain.

3. Michael Brown argues that gay priests will most likely fail to keep their vows of chastity once they are living together in a seminary and that this is a good reason to prevent gay men from becoming priests. Meanwhile, James Martin believes that gay men should become priests, specifically because they are willing to sacrifice themselves to enter a church that does not approve of their sexual orientation. Which author's argument do you think is stronger? Why?

Chapter 2

1. Thomas Farrell contends that the US Supreme Court justices should not have used Catholic moral reasoning to decide a case that was in no way related to the Catholic faith. Do you think it is possible for justices to put aside their personal beliefs when making decisions, or do you think that justices' morals and beliefs should play a role when they are making a ruling? Explain your reasoning.

2. Tyler Anderson believes that Pope Francis was correct in advising Catholics not to have an abundance of children, for the world's resources are suffering from overpopulation. Do you agree with Anderson that the future of the planet trumps the right of parents to have as many children as they want? Why, or why not?

3. Donald Hanson argues that Catholics should oppose medical aid in dying because all life is precious and unique to God, who is the real owner of all human bodies. How do you evaluate Hanson's argument? Explain.

Chapter 3

1. Dan Delzell believes that prohibiting Catholic priests from marrying is a cruel form of spiritual abuse, for it denies priests the opportunity to seek joy and contentment with a spouse. Do you agree with Delzell's humanitarian view of the question of priestly celibacy, or should the sacrifice of loneliness that priests offer to God remain essential to the Catholic priesthood? Explain your reasoning.

2. Dwight Longenecker contends that the Catholic Church could not permit women to become priests even if it wanted to do so, for Jesus chose only male apostles, and the church cannot alter the substance of Christ's original sacrament. Do you agree with Longenecker that the church should look to Jesus's action as the foundation of a male-only tradition in the priesthood? Explain.

3. Do you agree with Jason Berry, as interviewed by Priyanka Boghani, that Pope Francis's devoted and sympathetic attitude toward victims of priestly sexual abuse signals his willingness to implement substantial church reforms that would fully prosecute all priests who commit acts of abuse? Should the pope's own intentions and actions be the only conduits of punishing such priests, or should the secular world have a say in the matter? Explain.

Chapter 4

1. Michael Brendan Dougherty argues that Pope Francis's participation in politics distorts the Catholic faith by bending religious doctrine to fit political policies. Do you agree that religious dogma should not change to suit changing social environments, or should religion grow and develop to remain relevant to the modern age? Explain.

2. Nicholas G. Hahn III believes that the diplomatic deal Pope Francis helped broker between the United States and Cuba was shortsighted in that it did not ask for democratic freedoms for the oppressed Cuban people. Is Hahn correct that in failing to do this, the pope let down his church, which takes a strong stance against human rights abuses? Is it right to blame the pope for the shortcomings of the deal, or should this responsibility fall on the shoulders of the involved politicians? Explain.

3. Ken Ham argues that Pope Francis is wrong to combine religious dogma and science by claiming that the big bang was required to bring about God's creation. According to Ham, the pope's statement implies that God's word is not perfect but must depend on the scientific advancements of humans for legitimacy. Do you think religious doctrine as written in the Bible should be taken at face value, or can human science complement faith? Explain your answer.

Organizations to Contact

The editors have compiled the following list of organizations concerned with the issues debated in this book. The descriptions are derived from materials provided by the organizations. All have publications or information available for interested readers. The list was compiled on the date of publication of the present volume; the information provided here may change. Be aware that many organizations take several weeks or longer to respond to inquiries, so allow as much time as possible.

Catholic Democrats
PO Box 6262, Boston, MA   02114
info@catholicdemocrats.org
website: www.catholicdemocrats.org

Catholic Democrats is a not-for-profit national organization representing a Catholic voice within the Democratic Party as well as a voice for the Democratic Party in the Catholic community. Through the "Issues" section of its website, Catholic Democrats shows how the positions of the Democratic Party are consistent with Catholic social teaching. Some of the topics presented on the website include abortion, immigration, the economy, health care, education, and the environment.

Catholic Health Association of the United States (CHA)
1875 Eye Street NW, Suite 1000, Washington, DC   20006
(202) 296-3993
e-mail: servicecenter@chausa.org
website: www.chausa.org

The Catholic Health Association of the United States (CHA) is the nation's largest group of nonprofit health care sponsors, systems, and facilities. With six hundred hospitals and fourteen hundred long-term care facilities across the United States, CHA provides health care to patients of all ages, races, and religious beliefs. CHA publishes the semimonthly newsletter

Catholic Health World, the bimonthly professional journal *Health Progress*, and the quarterly newsletter *Health Care Ethics USA*. It also provides the *News Release Digest*, a weekly collection of news releases from across the ministry.

Catholic Relief Services (CRS)

228 W. Lexington Street, Baltimore, MD   21201
(888) 277-7575
website: www.crs.org

Catholic Relief Services (CRS) is a humanitarian agency that provides assistance to 130 million people in more than one hundred countries in Africa, Asia, Latin America, the Middle East, and Eastern Europe. CRS is a pro-life organization dedicated to preserving the sacredness and dignity of human life from conception to natural death. The organization works to promote human development by responding to major emergencies, fighting disease and poverty, and nurturing peaceful and just societies around the world. Its website offers a link to the CRS Newswire and access to its blog, which features entries such as "Pope Francis Calls for 'Change of Paradigm' in Ending World Hunger."

Catholics for Choice (CFC)

1436 U Street NW, Suite 301, Washington, DC   20009-3997
(202) 986-6093 • fax: (202) 332-7995
e-mail: cfc@catholicsforchoice.org
website: www.catholicsforchoice.org

Founded in 1973, Catholics for Choice (CFC) supports a woman's moral and legal right to follow her conscience in matters of sexuality, reproductive freedom, and reproductive health. It conducts education and advocacy work in the United States, Europe, and Latin America. CFC is an accredited non-governmental organization in the United Nations (UN) system and has participated in numerous UN conferences and forums. The CFC website offers articles, press releases, op-eds, and podcasts, as well as access to past issues of *Conscience*, CFC's quarterly magazine.

Catholics in Alliance for the Common Good (CACG)

1612 K Street, Suite 400, Washington, DC 20006
(202) 499-4968
info@catholicsinalliance.org
website: www.catholicsinalliance.org

Catholics in Alliance for the Common Good (CACG) is a nonprofit organization that promotes public policies and effective programs that enhance the inherent dignity of all, especially the poor and underserved. CACG conducts public policy analysis and advocacy, provides strategic media outreach, and engages citizens in the service of the common good. The CACG website offers press releases, links to news articles, access to the *Common Good Forum* blog, and access to the *Millennial* online journal, which features entries such as "The Promise and Limits of Finding the Common Ground on Abortion" and "Pope Francis' Ecology Encyclical: What Can We Expect?"

DignityUSA

PO Box 376, Medford, MA 02155
(202) 861-0017 • fax: (781) 397-0584
e-mail: info@dignityusa.org
website: www.dignityusa.org

DignityUSA has been advocating for change in the Catholic Church's teaching on homosexuality since 1969. DignityUSA envisions a time when gay, lesbian, bisexual, and transgender Catholics are affirmed and can participate fully in all aspects of life within the church and in society. DignityUSA publishes *Breath of the Spirit*, a weekly electronic newsletter; *Dateline*, a monthly newsletter; and *Quarterly Voice*, a quarterly publication for DignityUSA members.

Leadership Conference of Women Religious (LCWR)

8808 Cameron Street, Silver Spring, MD 20910
(301) 588-4955 • fax: (301) 587-4575
website: www.lcwr.org

The Leadership Conference of Women Religious (LCWR) is the association of Catholic women nuns and other religious groups in the United States. It has more than fifteen hundred members who represent more than 80 percent of women religious in America. In the LCWR Call for 2010–2015, LCWR members committed themselves to embracing critical change to honor an increasingly diverse membership within LCWR; preparing women religious for leadership in an emerging intercultural, global reality; and standing for social justice to establish economic equality, abolish modern-day slavery, and ensure immigrant rights. LCWR publications include the monthly *Update* newsletter, annual reports, and the journal *LCWR Occasional Papers.*

National Organization for Marriage (NOM)
2029 K Street NW, Washington, DC   20006
(888) 894-3604
e-mail: contact@nationformarriage.org
website: www.nationformarriage.org

Founded in 2007, the National Organization for Marriage (NOM) is a nonprofit organization dedicated to promoting an understanding of marriage as the union of one man and one woman. It is involved in organizing opposition to same-sex marriage–related initiatives in state and federal legislatures, in the courts at all levels, and in the general culture. NOM operates the NOM Education Fund, which organizes the yearly March for Marriage in Washington, DC, and the Marriage Anti-Defamation Alliance, which protects and defends the right of pro-marriage Americans to speak out on their convictions. The NOM website includes press releases, the *NOM Blog*, study results, research briefs, and talking points on defending marriage.

Pax Christi International
Rue du Vieux Marché aux Grains, 21, Brussels   B1000
   Belgium
++32 (0)2 502 55 50 • fax: ++32 (0)2 502 46 26
website: www.paxchristi.net

Pax Christi International is a nonprofit, nongovernmental Catholic peace movement working on a global scale on a wide variety of issues in the fields of human rights, human security, disarmament, demilitarization, just world order, religion, and violent conflict. The organization was founded in 1945 as a way to bring about peace in Europe after World War II. More than seventy years later, Pax Christi has more than one hundred member organizations active in more than fifty countries and five continents worldwide. Its website offers an archive of its monthly newsletter and access to its blog, *Pax Christi Peace Stories.*

Pew Research Center Religion and Public Life Project
1615 L Street NW, Suite 700, Washington, DC   20036
(202) 419-4300 • fax: (202) 419-4349
website: www.pewforum.org

The Pew Research Center is a "fact tank" that conducts public opinion polls and social science research; reports and analyzes news; and holds forums and briefings. Pew's Religion and Public Life project seeks to promote a deeper understanding of issues at the intersection of religion and public affairs. It pursues its mission by delivering timely, impartial information but does not take positions on policy debates. At the Religion and Public Life project website are articles such as "In U.S., Pope's Popularity Continues to Grow," "The Global Catholic Population," and "'Strong' Catholic Identity at Four-Decade Low in U.S."

United States Conference of Catholic Bishops (USCCB)
3211 Fourth Street NE, Washington, DC   20017
(202) 541-3000
website: www.usccb.org

The United States Conference of Catholic Bishops (USCCB) is the official organization of the Catholic hierarchy in the United States. The purpose of the conference is to promote the programs and biblical interpretations of the church and carry out education and advocacy on various social issues based on church doctrine and guidance. The USCCB website offers a link to the Catholic News Service, featuring articles such as "Reason for Pope's Popularity Seen Not Only in Message but in His Example." The website also offers press releases and reports, as well as access to the USCCB blog, Facebook page, and Twitter feed.

Bibliography of Books

John L. Allen Jr.   *Against the Tide: The Radical Leadership of Pope Francis.* Ligouri, MO: Ligouri Publications, 2014.

John L. Allen Jr.   *The Catholic Church: What Everyone Needs to Know.* New York: Oxford University Press, 2014.

John L. Allen Jr.   *The Francis Miracle: Inside the Transformation of the Pope and the Church.* New York: Time, 2015.

R. Scott Appleby and Kathleen Sprows Cummings, eds.   *Catholics in the American Century: Recasting Narratives of U.S. History.* Ithaca, NY: Cornell University Press, 2012.

Jason Berry   *Render unto Rome: The Secret Life of Money in the Catholic Church.* New York: Broadway Books, 2012.

Dom Arturo Cattaneo, ed.   *Married Priests? 30 Crucial Questions About Celibacy.* San Francisco, CA: Ignatius Press, 2012.

Eamon Duffy   *Saints and Sinners: A History of the Popes.* 4th ed. New Haven, CT: Yale University Press, 2015.

Anthony Esolen   *Reclaiming Catholic Social Teaching: A Defense of the Church's True Teachings on Marriage, Family, and the State.* Manchester, NH: Sophia Institute Press, 2014.

Antonio Gaspari *A Cyclone Named Francis: The Pope Who Came from the Ends of the Earth*. New York: Zenit Books, 2014.

James Hitchcock *History of the Catholic Church: From the Apostolic Age to the Third Millennium*. San Francisco, CA: Ignatius Press, 2012.

Austen Ivereigh *The Great Reformer: Francis and the Making of a Radical Pope*. New York: Henry Holt, 2014.

Christopher Kaczor *The Seven Big Myths About the Catholic Church: Distinguishing Fact from Fiction About Catholicism*. San Francisco, CA: Ignatius Press, 2012.

Walter Kasper *The Catholic Church: Nature, Reality and Mission*. New York: Bloomsbury, 2015.

Jeffrey A. Krames *Lead with Humility: 12 Leadership Lessons from Pope Francis*. New York: AMACOM, 2014.

Chris Lowney *Pope Francis: Why He Leads the Way He Leads*. Chicago, IL: Loyola Press, 2013.

Patricia Miller *Good Catholics: The Battle over Abortion in the Catholic Church*. Los Angeles: University of California Press, 2014.

Diane Moczar *The Church Under Attack: Five Hundred Years That Split the Church and Scattered the Flock*. Manchester, NH: Sophia Institute Press, 2013.

Diane Moczar   *Seven Lies About Catholic History: Infamous Myths About the Church's Past and How to Answer Them.* Charlotte, NC: TAN Books, 2010.

John W. O'Malley   *A History of the Popes: From Peter to the Present.* Lanham, MD: Rowman and Littlefield, 2010.

Jo Piazza   *If Nuns Ruled the World: Ten Sisters on a Mission.* New York: Open Road, 2014.

Elisabetta Piqué   *Pope Francis: Life and Revolution: A Biography of Jorge Bergoglio.* Chicago, IL: Loyola Press, 2014.

Pope Francis   *The Church of Mercy: A Vision for the Church.* Chicago, IL: Loyola Press, 2014.

Margaret Nutting Ralph   *Why the Catholic Church Must Change: A Necessary Conversation.* Lanham, MD: Rowman and Littlefield, 2013.

Francis Rooney   *The Global Vatican: An Inside Look at the Catholic Church, World Politics, and the Extraordinary Relationship Between the United States and the Holy See.* Lanham, MD: Rowman and Littlefield, 2013.

Russell Shaw   *American Church: The Remarkable Rise, Meteoric Fall, and Uncertain Future of Catholicism in America.* San Francisco, CA: Ignatius Press, 2013.

Christian Smith, Kyle Longest, Jonathan Hill, and Kari Christoffersen — *Young Catholic America: Emerging Adults In, Out of, and Gone from the Church*. New York: Oxford University Press, 2014.

John Vidmar — *The Catholic Church Through the Ages: A History*. 2nd ed. Mahwah, NJ: Paulist Press, 2014.

Benjamin Wiker — *The Catholic Church & Science: Answering the Questions, Exposing the Myths*. Charlotte, NC: TAN Books, 2011.

Garry Wills — *The Future of the Catholic Church with Pope Francis*. New York: Viking, 2015.

Thomas E. Woods and Antonio Canizares — *How the Catholic Church Built Western Civilization*. Washington, DC: Regnery, 2012.

Index

A

Abortifacients, 75, 82
Abortion
  ban amendment hearings, 93
  Catholic health care providers,
    86, 87–89
  Catholic opposition, 81, 86–
    89, 92–93, 159–160
  pro-choice Catholics' role in
    debate, 90–94
Abuse scandal. *See* Sexual abuse
Active euthanasia, 108
Aid in dying/assisted suicide, 107–
  108, 109, 111–112
AIDS and HIV, 155
Air quality, 103
Alito, Samuel, 77, 82
Altar servers, 117
American College of Obstetricians
  and Gynecologists, 97
American-Cuban relations
  Cuban dissident voices, and
    Pope Francis, 173–176
  new diplomacy, and Pope
    Francis, 169–172
American Public Health Associa-
  tion, 112
Anderson, Tyler, 101–105
Anglican Church
  contraception, 166
  history, 139
  ordination of women, 130,
    131–132, 133, 138–139
Argentina, 149, 176
Aristotle, 84

Assisted suicide. *See* Aid in dying/
  assisted suicide
Asthma, 103
Astronomy, 154
Augustine of Hippo, 194–195, 197

B

Ban Ki-moon, 179
Beale, Stephen, 118–122
Beisner, Calvin, 183, 185
Benedict XVI
  AIDS epidemic, 155
  clergy sex abuse scandal
    policy, 148
  contraception, 155
  gay marriage, 59
  gay priests, 58
  personality, 165, 168
  politics during papacy, 174
  See also Ratzinger, Joseph
Benson, Robert Hugh, 167
Bergoglio, Jorge Mario. *See* Francis
Berry, Jason, 147, 148–151
Bible
  commentaries and exegesis,
    195
  creation stories, 189, 191, 192,
    196
  God's word and unchange-
    ability, 191–192
  homosexuality, 19
  human life, 107–108
  literalism dangers, 195
  marriage/celibacy, 121, 124,
    126, 127
  prayer, 121, 158

Big bang theory
  Pope Francis is wrong to support, 188, 189, 191–192
  Pope Francis's support aligns with Catholicism, 190, 193–197
  proposal, 190
Birth control. *See* Contraception
Bishops. *See* Cardinals and bishops
Body, and consideration of life's value, 106, 107–108
Boghani, Priyanka, 147–151
Bourgeois, Roy, 139
Braschi, Romulo Antonio, 134
Brown, Michael, 57–62
Burke, Raymond Leo, 27–31, 117
Burwell, Conestoga Wood Specialties v. (2014), 75
Burwell v. Hobby Lobby Stores, Inc. (2014), 75, 77, 80, 81–85
Business structures, 75, 77, 78

C

Cahill, Jane Furlong, 93
California, Catholic Church of, 144
Canon law
  inadequate justice mechanism, 150
  priestly celibacy, 125, 126, 127
Capitalism, 169, 172
Carasik, Lauren, 141–146
Cardinals and bishops, 14
  clergy sex abuse scandal, 145–146, 149, 150–151
  contraception and abortion, 72, 73, 93
  duties, for the pope, 167–168
  opinions on gay Catholics, 27, 28–31, 53–54, 61
  support of universal health care, 72–73
  women in the priesthood, 117, 133–134
Carey, George, 134
Castro, Raúl, 174, 176
Catechism of the Catholic Church, 58–59, 66–67, 133, 162–163
Catholic Church history, 15–16
Catholic hospitals, 87–88
Catholic moral reasoning, in legal decisions, 80–85
Catholic politicians, 53, 182, 186
Catholic populations
  everyday Catholics vs. church leadership, 51, 53–56, 93, 94, 98t
  statistics, 14, 186
Catholics for a Free Choice, 91, 93–94
Celibacy
  priests should be allowed to marry, 123–127
  priests should remain celibate, 110–122
  same-sex-attracted men and priests, 61–62, 66–67
  as tradition/canon law, 125, 126, 127
Charities, funding, 45, 47–50
Chastity. *See* Celibacy
Children
  child-centric arguments against gay marriage, 41–42
  procreation as purpose of (heterosexual) marriage, 32, 37
Cholij, Roman, 121, 122
Christianity, history, 14–15, 16

Chua, Bicbic, 99

Church hierarchy, 14, 144, 149

Church of England
contraception, 166
history, 139
ordination of women, 130,
131–132, 133, 138–139

Civil marriage, 33, 34, 35, 40

Clerical abuse scandal. *See* Sexual
abuse

Climate change
deniers' opinions and political
action, 177–180, 182–183,
185–187
Pope Francis displays ethics in
combatting, 181–187
Pope Francis is wrong to
combat, 177–179

Clinton, Bill, 40

Cohabitation, 29

Cold War, 172, 175

Communal living, 57, 62

Communism, 169, 170–172, 173

*Compendium of the Social Doctrine
of the Church*, 161

Conception, 81

Condoms, 155

*Conestoga Wood Specialties v. Bur-
well* (2014), 75

Congregation for Catholic Education, 61

Conscience exemptions and laws,
78, 87–89

Constantine, 15

Contraception
Affordable Care Act coverage,
and Catholic opposition, 72,
73, 74, 80, 81
availability and programs,
98–99, 104
Catholics' desires and public
opinion, 97–98, 98t, 99–100

Catholics' predictions, 98t
history of Catholic opposition, 92–93, 155, 165–166
vs. natural family planning,
95, 96–97, 100

Conversion, religious
Christian history, 15, 16
prayer, 158

Cooperation in evil, 82–85, 88

Copernicus, Nicolaus, 154

Cornwall Alliance for the Stewardship of Creation, 183, 185–186

Corporation business structure,
and religious rights, 75, 77, 78,
81–82

Counter-Reformation, 16

Creation
Biblical exegesis, 195
God's power considered, 139,
189, 191, 196
heliocentric vs. earth-centric
theory, 154
human life, 107–108
man and woman, 29
Pope Francis is wrong to support big bang theory, 188,
189, 191–192
Pope Francis's support of big
bang theory aligns with Catholicism, 190, 193–197
See also Environmental values;
Evolution

Creationism. *See* Evolution

Crusades, 15–16

Cuba
dissident voices and Pope
Francis's "deaf ears," 173–176
papal visits, 171, 174
Pope Francis is correct on
new American-Cuban rela-
tions, 169–172

Culp-Ressler, Tara, 95–100

D

Darwin, Charles, 155
Davenport, Coral, 184
David, 157
Davis, Henry, 82
Death, as part of life, 109
Death with dignity movement
    Catholics should not oppose,
        110–113
    opposes Catholic teaching,
        106–109
DeBernardo, Francis, 22–26
Defense of Marriage Act (1996),
    40
Delzell, Dan, 123–127
Democratic Party, 162
Deniers, climate change, 177–180,
    182–183, 185–187
Detachment, 122
DignityUSA, 19–20, 65
Diplomacy. *See* Religion in politics
Disciples, 128, 131, 132, 133
Discrimination. *See* Religious dis-
    crimination
Divorce and remarriage, 28
Doerflinger, Richard M., 86–89
Dolan, Timothy, 53–54, 61, 67, 72
Donnelly, Larry, 39–44
Dorris, Barbara, 143
Dougherty, Michael Brendan, 164–
    168
Duddy-Burke, Marianne, 65
Duvalier, Jean-Claude "Baby Doc,"
    48

E

Elections, popes, 138, 140
Employment. *See* Hiring and em-
    ployment; Labor rights

Ensoulment, 92
Environmental values
    overpopulation awareness,
        101, 102–105
    Pope Francis is ethical in
        combatting climate change,
        181–187
    Pope Francis is wrong to
        combat climate change, 177–
        180
    Pope Francis's focus, 17, 101,
        102, 178, 179, 181, 182–183,
        186–187
    stewardship concept, 179, 181
Episcopal Church, 130, 131, 138
Establishment Clause objections
    and related cases, 75–76, 78
Euthanasia, 108, 111
    See also Aid in dying/assisted
        suicide
Evangelical Protestantism
    abortion and contraception,
        75, 82, 83
    anti-environmental groups,
        183–186
Evil, cooperation, 82–85, 88
Evolution, 155
    Pope Francis is wrong to sup-
        port, 188, 189, 191–192
    Pope Francis's support aligns
        with Catholicism, 190, 193–
        197

F

Family planning
    Pope Francis correct to en-
        courage conservative plan-
        ning, 101–105
    Pope Francis's comments as
        misguided, 95–100
    Pope Francis's comments as
        political, 165–166

Family size
    and awareness of global over-
        population, 101, 102–105
    and family economics, 95, 96,
        98–99
Family structure, as building block
    of society, 37, 158
Farrell, Thomas, 80–85
Fatherhood, spiritual, 119–120
Federal contracting rules, 46
Federal funding, religious organi-
    zations, 45, 47–50
Female priests. *See* Women as
    priests
Ferraro, Geraldine, 93
Fiedler, Maureen, 137, 140
Food resources, 103
For-profit corporations, and reli-
    gious rights, 75, 77, 78, 81–82
Foreign aid, 165
Fossil fuels, 177, 178, 181, 185
Fournier, Keith, 156–163
Francis
    acceptance, gay Catholics, 20,
        22–26, 27–31, 58, 59
    clergy sex abuse scandal
        policy, 145–146, 147, 148–
        151
    creation and evolution, 188–
        192, 193–197
    Cuba visit and relations, 169–
        172, 173–176
    environmental values, 178,
        181, 182–183, 184, 186–187
    family planning, 95–100, 165–
        166
    gay marriage, 59
    gay priests, 58, 61
    is ethical in combatting cli-
        mate change, 181–187
    is wrong to combat climate
        change, 177–180
    personality, 165, 167, 168, 172,
        184
    political participation, and
        global social issues, 17, 155,
        157–158, 163, 164, 165–168,
        169–187
    priestly celibacy, 126, 127
    women priests, 134, 138, 139,
        140
Freedom
    Cuba, 173, 174–176
    human rights and true free-
        dom, 159, 161, 162

G

Galileo, 154
Gay Catholics
    celibacy, 61–62, 66–67
    pastoral care guidelines, 55
    place in the church, 51, 52–56
    Pope Francis's welcoming,
        opposition, 27–31
    Pope Francis's welcoming,
        questioning/debate, 58, 59
    Pope Francis's welcoming,
        support and outcomes, 20,
        22–26
Gay marriage
    Catholic Church opposition,
        20–21, 22, 32–38, 59
    Catholics may support, 39–44
    international votes, 40, 43–44,
        43*t*
    public opinion, 24*t*, 33, 37–38,
        40–41, 43*t*, 51, 53, 98*t*
    world religions' stances, 36
Gay priests
    church should not discrimi-
        nate against gays, 63–69

church should not ordain
gays, 57–62

particular difficulties, 60, 64,
65–66, 69

Gay rights movement, 19–20,
52–53

Gays and lesbians. *See* Gay Catholics; Gay priests; Gay rights
movement; Homosexuality

Ginsburg, Ruth Bader, 84

Glatz, Carol, 196

Global warming

deniers' opinions and political
action, 177–180, 182–183,
185–187

Pope Francis is ethical in
combatting, 181–187

Pope Francis is wrong to
combat, 177–179

God

God's word, unchangeability,
188, 191–192

human creation in God's image, 163

representation, liturgy, 131–
132

See also Jesus Christ

Goodstein, Laurie, 184

Gore, Al, 180

Gospels, 140

Government funding of religious
organizations, 48–50

Grassi, Julio César, 149

Greek philosophy, 194

Gregory IX, 16

Griffin, Leslie C., 82, 84

Gross, Alan, 174

H

Hahn, Nicholas G., III, 173–176

Ham, Ken, 188–192

Hanson, Donald, 106–109

Health care benefits and providers

Catholic opposition to abortion, 87–89

Catholic opposition to contraception, 72, 73, 74, 80, 81

Catholic support of universal
health care, 72–73

Obamacare discriminates
against Catholicism and
other religions, 74–79

Health care sharing ministries, 76

Heaven, 122

Heliocentric theory of the universe, 154

Heresy, 16, 154

Heritage Foundation, 186

Herwick, Edgar B., 190

Hiring and employment

Catholic organizations should
uphold rights of gays, 56

Catholic organizations
shouldn't be forced to hire
gays, 45–50

See also Health care benefits
and providers

Hitchens, Christopher, 48

HIV and AIDS, 155

*Hobby Lobby Stores, Inc., Burwell
v.* (2014), 75, 77, 80, 81–85

Homosexuality

Catholic Church history and
Catechism, 19–21, 58–59,
66–67, 145

Catholic Church stances,
changes and evolution, 20–
21, 22–26, 27–31

"passing" as straight, 65–66
public opinion, 24*t*, 53
as "suffering," 28, 29–30, 59
See also Gay Catholics; Gay
marriage; Gay priests
Human rights, 159
Convention on the Rights of
the Child, 142–143, 144
Cuban activism, 173, 174–176
papal encyclicals, 72–73
valuing life and, 88
Hunt, Mary, 94
Hyde/Weldon appropriations bill,
87

I

Immigration ministries, 48
Inclusivity
Christian history, 14–15
gay Catholics, 20, 22–26, 27–
31, 53
Income inequality, 182
Inquisitions, 16, 154
Intelligent design movement, 196–
197
International law, 142–143, 144
Ireland, gay marriage, 40, 42, 43–
44, 43*t*

J

Jenkins, Jack, 126
Jerusalem, 15–16
Jesuits (order), 176
See also Francis
Jesus Christ
celibacy, and priests' identifi-
cation, 118, 119, 120–121,
126
Christian faith, 14–15, 124

disciples and followers, 128,
131, 132, 133, 136, 140
sacraments, 132–133
suffering and death, 109, 120–
121
teachings and values, 182, 186
John Paul II
apology, Galileo, 154
clergy sexual abuse scandal,
150–151
contraception, 165
health care and human rights,
73
homosexuality, 20
politics during papacy, 172,
174
priestly celibacy, 119, 120
women priests, 133–134, 137
John XXIII, 72–73, 119
Jordan, Mark D., 64
Justin Martyr, 194

K

Kane, Theresa, 137–138
Kasper, Walter, 28
King, Martin Luther, Jr., 161
Kissling, Frances, 94
Koch, Charles and David, 179,
182, 183, 185–187

L

Labor rights, 184
Ladies in White (activist
movement), 174, 175
Larson v. Valente (1982), 76, 78
Law, Bernard, 149
Lemaître, George, 190
Leo XIII, 184

"Letter from Birmingham Jail" (King), 161
Levite priests, 122
Lewis, C.S., 130, 131–132
Li Tim-Oi, Florence, 130
Lipka, Michael, 98*t*
Literalism, scripture readings, 195
Little Sisters of the Poor, 75, 78
Lombardi, Federico, 28
Loneliness, 120–121
Longenecker, Dwight, 128–135
Lord of the World (Benson), 167
Lucente, Thomas, 193–197
Lumetzberger, Christine Mayr, 129, 134
Luther, Martin, 16
Lynch, Mary, 137

M

Mahony, Roger M., 145–146, 149
Making Gay Okay: How Rationalizing Homosexual Behavior Is Changing Everything (Reilly), 46–47
Marriage
    heterosexual, 32, 33–34
    history and human nature, 33, 34–35
    indissolubility, 28, 29
    personal experiences, 42–43
    priesthood compared, 68–69, 119, 121
    priests, opposition, 118–122
    priests, support, 98*t*, 117, 123–127
    See also Gay marriage
Martin, James, 60, 63–69
Mary Magdalene, 140

Massachusetts, gay marriage, 41–42
Materialism, 159
Maynard, Brittany, 107, 108, 111
McQuillan, Patricia, 91–92
Medieval Inquisition, 16, 154
Miller, Patricia, 90–94
Misogyny, 92–93
Moral and Pastoral Theology (Davis), 82
Moral reasoning
    Catholic moral reasoning used by US Supreme Court, 80, 82–85
    relativism vs. moral truths, 159
Morano, Marc, 177–180
Mother Teresa, 48
Murdoch, Rupert, 179

N

National Catholic Welfare Council, 72–73
Natural family planning, 95, 96, 97, 100
New Testament
    God's word, 191–192
    homosexuality, 19
    human life, 107–108
    marriage/celibacy, 121, 124, 126, 127
    prayer, 121, 158
    See also Jesus Christ
No Taxpayer Funding for Abortion Act (bill), 87
Nuns, 137–138
Nussbaum, L. Martin, 74–79

O

Obama, Barack
Cuba relations, 175–176
federal contracting rules, 46, 49, 50
gay marriage, 40
See also Patient Protection and Affordable Care Act (2010)
O'Brien, Jon, 94
O'Connor, John, 93
Old Testament
commentaries and exegesis, 195
creation stories, 189, 192, 196
David's leadership, 157
homosexuality, 19
priests, 122
Olvera, Robert, 110–113
Ordination
church should not discriminate against gay priests, 63–69
church should not ordain gay priests, 57–62
rates, and priest shortage, 68, 116
sacramental nature of priesthood, 131–133
women, history, 129, 130, 134, 137, 138–139
women should be allowed to be priests, 136–140
women should never be allowed to be priests, 128–135
Oregon, assisted suicide, 107, 111
Oreskes, Naomi, 179, 180
O'Rourke, Joseph, 93
Orthodox Christian Church, 15

Overpopulation, 101, 102–105, 165–166

P

Palliative care, 109, 113
Palumbo, Robert, 65
Papacy. *See* Popes and papacy
Papal encyclicals
climate and environment, 178, 183, 184
human rights, 72–73
labor, 184
laws of God/contraception, 166
priests, 119, 120
Paprocki, Thomas J., 32–38
Parrilla, Bruno Rodríguez, 171
"Passing" as heterosexual, 65–66
Passive euthanasia, 108
Pastoral programs, gay Catholics, 23, 25
Patient Protection and Affordable Care Act (2010)
Catholics should not argue with moral reasoning, 80–85
contraception inclusion, Catholic opposition, 72, 73, 74, 80, 81
discriminates against Catholicism and other religions, 74–79
religious classifications, details, 76, 78–79
Paul, and Pauline literature
on human life, 107–108
on marriage/celibacy, 121, 124, 126
Paul's spread of the word, 37–38
on prayer, 121, 158

Paul VI, 119, 120, 122, 155, 165–166

Pavone, Frank, 14

Peter, 15

Petroleum industry, 182, 185–187

Philippines, family planning, 96, 97–99, 100, 165–166

Philosophy, Greek, 194

Piazza, Jo, 136–140

Pius X, 119, 122

Pius XI, 48, 119, 120

Pius XII, 122, 190

Plante, Thomas G., 68

Plato, 194

Poggioli, Sylvia, 145

Political parties, 161–162

Politics. See Religion in politics

Pontifical Academy of Sciences, 179, 194, 196

Poor, working and caring for
climate change effects, 184
Jesus's focus, 182
overpopulation and poverty, 97–98, 99, 103
political funding, 47
political participation, 155, 159
Pope Francis's focus, 155, 170, 182, 184

Pope Francis. See Francis

Popes and papacy
church hierarchy, 14, 144, 149
church history, 15
elections, 138, 140
fiction, 167
political history, 15–17, 142
See also specific Popes

Population. See Catholic populations; Overpopulation

Prayer
priests, time devoted, 121
for those in politics, 158
vocations, 139

Priesand, Sally J., 138

Priests
calls, and decisions about the priesthood, 117, 124–125, 129, 139
celibacy's value, 118–122
clergy abuse scandal, 141–146, 147–151
duties, 116
gay men should not be discriminated against, 63–69
gay men should not be ordained, 57–62
marriage, public opinion, 98t, 117
marriage history, 122, 126
marriage should be allowed, 123–127
population/totals, and shortage statistics, 68, 116–117
sacramental nature of priesthood, 131–133
women, history, 129, 130, 134, 137, 138–139
women, public opinion, 98t, 117, 139
women should be allowed to be, 136–140
women should never be allowed to be, 128–135

Principle of cooperation in evil, 82–85, 88

Pro-choice Catholics, 90–94

Pro-life values, 155, 159–160
anti-abortion, 86–89
anti-contraception, 72, 73, 81, 155

medical interventions and technologies, 73, 75, 109
Pope Francis, 17
vs. right to die movement, 106, 107–109
Procreative value of marriage, 32, 37
Protestantism, 16
  creationism vs. evolution, 194–195
  Protestant Reformation, 16
  See also Evangelical Protestantism
Public opinion
  changes desired in the church, 98*t*, 117, 137
  contraception, 97–98, 99–100
  gay marriage, 24*t*, 33, 37–38, 40–41, 43*t*, 51, 53, 98*t*
  homosexuality, 24*t*, 53
  religion in politics, 160*t*
  women priests, 98*t*, 139

Q

Quinn, Donna, 140

R

Rabbis, 138
Ratzinger, Joseph, 133–134, 159
  See also Benedict XVI
Reason, 193, 194–195, 197
Rees, Martin, 179
Reilly, Robert, 46–47
Relativism, 159
Religion in politics
  Catholic Church need not participate in politics, 164–168, 176

Catholic Church should participate in politics, 156–163
political funding, and ethical conflicts, 48–50
political nature and power of the Vatican, 14, 15–16, 142
Pope Francis's action and influence, 17, 155, 157–158, 163, 164, 165–168, 169, 170–177
public opinion, 160*t*
secularism and church history, 14, 16, 154
Religious discrimination
  arguments against gay priests, 57, 61–62, 64–65
  Catholic institutions should not be forced to hire gays, 45–50
  Catholic leadership should stop discriminating against gays, 51–56
  church should not discriminate against gay priests, 63–69
Religious Freedom Restoration Act (1993), 75, 76, 77
Religious liberty
  abortion, 87–89
  church doctrine, 145
  conscience exemptions and laws, 78, 87–89
  contraception, legal cases, 75–76, 80–85, 94
  political participation, 158
Republican Party, 162, 182, 185, 186
Right to die. *See* Death with dignity movement
Rmuse, 181–187
Rocca, Francis X., 133
Roe v. Wade (1973), 91, 92

Roman Catholic Church, 15
Roman Catholic Womenpriests, 134
Roman Inquisition, 16, 154
Rossetti, Stephen, 67
Rubio, Marco, 175–176
Ruether, Rosemary Radford, 92–93
Ruiz, Albor, 171
Ruiz, Julio, 171

S

Sachs, Jeffrey, 179
Sacraments, 132–133
    See also Marriage; Ordination
Sacrifice
    celibacy as, 118, 120
    gay priests' unique issues, 69
    Jesus Christ, 109, 120
Same-sex marriage. See Gay marriage
Schellnhuber, Hans Joachim, 179
Scicluna, Charles J., 145
Scientific discovery and theory
    Catholic Church disputes and history, 16, 154–155
    Catholic Church's support of science, 155, 188–192, 193–197
    See also Climate change
Sebelius, Kathleen, 75
Secularism and Catholic Church influence. See Religion in politics
Self-love, 26
Sexual abuse
    accountability and punishment of abusers, 137, 141, 143, 146, 147, 149–150, 151
    church is progressing toward clerical abuse reform, 147–151

church's stance was not strong enough, 141–146
    cover-ups, 65–66, 137, 142–143, 145
    effects on the priesthood, 117
    scapegoating and blame of gay clergy, 61, 62, 64–65
    victims, 142–143, 144, 146, 148–149, 150–151
Smith, Margaret, 64
Social justice endeavors
    political ways and means, 155, 156, 159
    Pope Francis's focus, 155, 170
    universal health care, 72–73
Soler, Berta, 174, 175
Spectrum of sexuality, 66
Stanford, Peter, 129, 134
Stiglitz, Joseph, 179
Supreme Court cases
    abortion, 91, 92
    Establishment Clause, 76, 78
    religious freedom, 75, 76, 77, 80, 81–85
Supreme Court justices, 81–82, 82–83, 84
Survivors Network of Those Abused by Priests, 143, 151
Sweeney, Kevin J., 68
Synod on the Family, 28–29, 30

T

Taboola, 51–56
"Theistic evolution," 155
Tomasi, Silvano, 143
Truth-telling, 26

U

United Nations
climate science policy, 178, 179, 180, 183
Committee on the Rights of the Child/Convention on the Rights of the Child, 142–143, 144, 145, 146
Universe creation. *See* Big bang theory
Urban II, 15–16
US Conference of Catholic Bishops, 53–54, 55, 72, 93
US Department of Health and Human Services (HHS), 75, 77

V

Valente, Larson v. (1982), 76, 78
Vatican City and Holy See
political history and nature, 14, 15–16, 142
political participation under Pope Francis, 165–168
sexual abuse scandal management, 142, 143, 144, 145, 149–150
Vicuña, Rafael, 195–197
Vitello, Paul, 64, 65, 67
Vocations to the priesthood, 117, 124–125, 129, 139

W

Wadhams, Peter, 179
Walsh, Mary Ann, 145

Water resources, 103
Wesolowski, Józef, 150
Westen, John-Henry, 58–59, 61
Wineke, William R., 169–172
Women
empowerment, contraception and smaller family size, 96, 97
reproductive rights, and church history, 92–93
roles in the church, 117, 130–132, 135, 136, 137–138, 140
world religions, leadership, 130, 138–139
See also Women as priests
Women as priests
growing the priesthood, 117, 130, 139
history, 129, 130, 134, 137, 138–139
public opinion, 98*t*, 117, 139
removal of clergy in favor of, 139, 145
should be allowed, 136–140
should never be allowed, 128–135

Y

Young Catholics
altar servers, 117
opinions, 24*t*

Z

Zmirak, John, 45–50